# SCRATCH-BUILT BUILDINGS

Written & Photographed
By
## Paul Bason

From the publishers of
## BRITISH RAILWAY MODELLING

Warners Group Publications Plc.,
The Maltings, West Street, Bourne, Lincolnshire PE10 9PH
Phone: 01778 391027 • Fax: 01778 425437

# •SCRATCH-BUILT BUILDINGS•

In this, the fourth book in the *British Railway Modelling* series, I hope to give the reader a practical insight into the 'art' of scratch-building structures predominantly from plastic card. If you have had a chance to look at my first book, *Lineside Buildings* (also published by the *British Railway Modelling* team), you will, I hope, already have an idea of how the aspiring model maker can progress from using ready-made buildings, through the various realms of kit construction, and on to populate his or her layout with structures made using the highly rewarding pastime of scratch-building.

The aim of *Scratch-Built Buildings* is therefore, to expand and move the topic

*Paul Bason* has over many years won acclaim for his scratch-building skills, having gained first place in many competitions for his 4mm scale cottages scratch-built from plastic card and for scratch-building EM gauge locomotives from brass as well. It is no surprise, therefore, that Paul's models, photographs and reviews have been a regular feature in the pages of British Railway Modelling since its very first issue over fifteen years ago. In real life Paul is a chartered quantity surveyor working for a large multi-national construction cost and management consultancy and is a keen railway photographer in his spare time.

stage-by-stage photographs, and a host of annotated three-dimensional drawings in an attempt to reveal just how easy scratch-building can really be.

Although I normally use plastic card as a basis for most of my models, we will also, for comparison, have a brief look at using plywood as a structural alternative. Largely, as I model in EM, all of the models featured in these pages have been made in 4mm to 1foot scale but, if you want to make a building in another scale please don't be put off, I am confident that, with a little thought, the same basic techniques can be easily adapted to suit all of the other commonly modelled scales from 2mm through to 7mm.

Having started by reviewing just what you will need to start scratch-building, we then take a look at the ways you can research, survey and plan your model before focussing on the various elements of construction commonly found on a model building. To help and assist those who are new to both construction and scratch-building I have also included throughout the book, as a handy reference, a varied selection of real-life details taken from a host of prototypes that often need to be replicated in model form.

Between some of the sections you will find a variety of inspirational Prototype Projects that illustrate some of the building types that could easily add realism or interest to your layout. Before finishing the book with a look at painting and those ever important finishing touches, we explore the interesting, and often overlooked, topic of modelling thatched cottages. I know some readers will have the misapprehension that thatching is an extremely difficult process that only a few modellers can master, but believe me, it really isn't half as awkward as you might at first think. Just like most modelling processes, a few minutes planning and a little practice before you start will make all of the difference in the finished model.

So whether you need to make a cottage, a pub, a station or a shed I am sure that you will find something in this book to help and assist you with your project. Always remember that if someone else can do it, so can you, always be confident and, of course, don't be afraid to have a go. Whatever you do remember that you are participating in a fascinating hobby and, most importantly...

Have Fun

*Paul Bason*

forward such that the reader will be confident enough to attempt to model almost all of the common elements of construction that come together to make up most types of building found frequently along the lineside.

Once again I hope to explain my methods of construction, wherever possible, by illustrating the processes involved using a clear progression of

# WHY SCRATCH-BUILD?

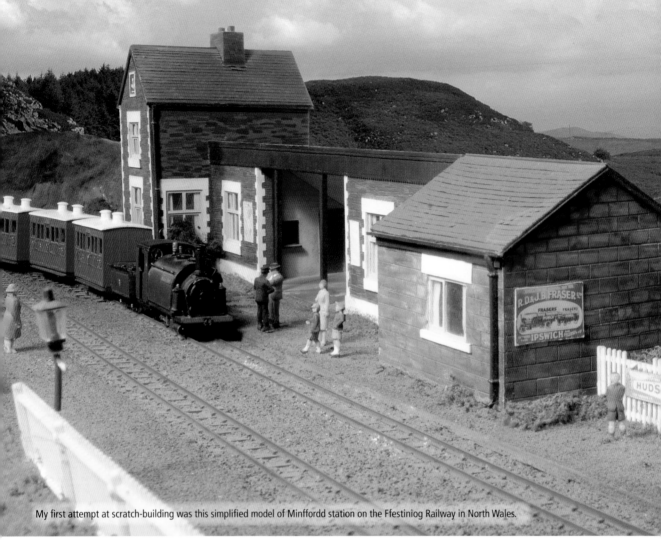

My first attempt at scratch-building was this simplified model of Minffordd station on the Ffestiniog Railway in North Wales.

This is a very good question indeed, and it is certainly one that I have often heard asked. Scratch-building, for the uninitiated, is basically the term used to describe the making of model buildings, or indeed any other scale models, from their basic components. In reality there are so many factors that influence a modeller's decision to have a go at scratch-building that it is extremely hard to categorise exactly why they do so. Some people, for example, tell me that they scratch-build because they cannot always buy exactly what they want and often wish for a more detailed model than those commercially available. Others may feel that it is easier and cheaper to scratch-build a structure or to make one fit exactly within a limited space rather than to purchase a kit and adapt it. Many modellers I have spoken to have already built plenty of card or plastic kits and just want to move on to something different. Maybe they feel the challenge of scratch-building will reveal a more interesting and rewarding side to the hobby. Arguably the most popular reason is that many modellers who turn to scratch-building, myself included, simply do so because they want to build a model of a specific prototype building and the only way they are going to get it is to make it themselves.

Regardless of the reason that makes you personally want to start scratch-building, the biggest hurdle I find most people come up against is to actually take the plunge and make those first

make a station building for my new narrow gauge layout, but being youthful (more likely impatient) and keen to learn, I decided to have a go on my own. To my surprise I was reasonably happy with the results, even though some of the details (such as the windows) are a bit coarse compared to my latest standards. My modelling experiment certainly pleased Dave, as it got him out of a job, and gave me a much needed confidence boost. As you might have guessed I soon became hooked and was planning my next building before the first was finished.

Having chatted with many would be scratch-builders while demonstrating this subject at shows in recent years, I know from experience that the main reason why people shy away from scratch-building as a whole is largely one of a lack of self-confidence. How many times have I heard 'Oh I couldn't do that', 'I haven't got the patience' or 'I just couldn't find the time to spend on such a complicated model'. Believe me, scratch-building isn't quite as hard as many envisage. It doesn't always need great levels of patience and, depending on the complexity of the structure

being modelled, doesn't have to take a great length of time to complete. I know it may sound obvious but I always encourage these people to;

• Always have confidence to at least try.

• Keep things simple, don't in the first instance attempt something so complicated that you will make a complete hash of it.

• Remember that most complicated tasks are only the result of a lot of smaller, simple ones.

• Always try out any new skill or method using scraps of materials before you do it for real.

• Practice will make perfect, don't worry even if you have to repeat a trial half a dozen times before you are satisfied with the results. Don't worry if you haven't picked up all of the skills overnight.

• Most importantly don't perpetually put off starting that long promised building – why not have a go, I'm sure you will be glad you did!

Before we take a look at the way I make buildings from plastic card it is well worthwhile considering some of the alternative materials and methods that can also be adopted.

The M&GNR station building at Wryde on the line from Peterborough to Wisbech was the subject of my second scratch-built project.

intrepid steps. I remember first learning the basics of the plastic card method of scratch-building when I joined a model railway club just after I left school in the late 1970s. My tutor, Dave Smith of 'Woodcroft' fame, was at the time experimenting with a scribed stone technique, having just finished a Highland Railway station building for his friend Brian Small, in which he had cut out and stuck on every individual stone from thin plastic sheet! At one time Dave was going to

This GNR signal box comprises a D&S etched kit for the windows and bargeboards but otherwise is made from scratch. A full account of how it was made can be found in *BRM*'s Book No.1 *Lineside Buildings* from the same author.

## Scratch-building Methods

When starting out, the newcomer to scratchbuilding is faced with the choice of several basic ways to build reasonably accurate buildings. The most commonly used methods I have experienced involve one or even a combination of the following:-

• Buildings constructed entirely from plastic card.

• Thick paper or card can be used for almost all of the structure.

• Balsa or card structure covered with brick paper.

• Embossed plastic card is often glued to a shell of plywood or thick card.

• Sheet metal such as brass can be used in association with commercially available etchings.

• Modelling clay such as 'Das' can be used for stone walls normally on a backing of thin plywood.

• Commercially manufactured building systems such as Langley's 'Masterbuild' range, Townstreet's range of components, and products such as 'Linka', although not strictly true scratch-building, offer the modeller a

halfway-house if you excuse the pun!

Although almost all of my model buildings have been scratch-built from plastic card. I will readily admit to having tried almost all of the methods listed above with varying degrees of success. I certainly take my hat off to those model builders who have mastered the art of using card, I don't know why, but I just could not get interested in modelling using this medium. I do however find the plastic faced plywood method very good for large buildings such as engine sheds that need a clear span over the tracks and have often used etched-brass components in conjunction with plastic to make a number of models, including a super-detailed signal box. The modelling clay method is well worth trying, particularly to represent some of the more rugged types of wall that are built in some areas of the country from large blocks of stone.

At the end of the day the method you chose is one of personal preference. I would certainly advocate the use of plastic card for most situations but I would still encourage any newcomer to the hobby to try as many methods as possible until he finds one that suits him and the type of buildings he, or she for that matter, wants to make.

For the record I find the main advantages of modelling buildings with plastic card to be:
• Plastic card is strong, easy to cut, very durable and inexpensive.
• A wide range of sheet thicknesses are readily available.
• Small section plastic strip can be bought in many sizes.
• Unusual shapes and sections are easy to get hold of.
• Brickwork can be bought as embossed sheets.
• There are a large number of injection-moulded components on the market that can be used to complement a basic model and make the scratch-building process a whole lot easier.

As I am sure you are already aware, model-makers are a very resourceful breed, I am often amused to hear what odd scraps and pieces of junk can be used to make the basis of a particular building. Plastic half-round guttering, for instance, makes an ideal base for a Dutch barn's roof, particularly if it is covered with some sort of corrugated sheeting. Perhaps the moral of this, if you can call it a moral, is not to be too rigid in your approach to model making, always look around you for handy scrap materials to use and certainly don't be afraid to experiment.

We now need to take a little time to plan just how to go about making a simple structure from scratch.

The late Alan Browning's fine Black Cat Brewery on Eastwell is a good example of a building made from plastic card around a plywood shell.

# ◦ TOOLS, PAINTS AND ADHESIVES ◦

A selection of tools needed for scratch-building structures.

If you already possess, or have read a copy of my first book for *BRM*, *Lineside Buildings*, you will have a good idea of which basic tools you will need to tackle a simple scratch-built building. If you haven't, here is a quick résumé of the most useful tools that you may need:

- Modelling knife
- A good supply of new blades
- Steel ruler or metal straight edge
- Razor saw
- A selection of small files
- Large flat and round files
- Propelling fibreglass brush
- Small pliers and cutters
- Small ordinary quality or old paint brushes for applying solvent
- Cutting mat (I use an A3 sized one)

- A pin vice
- A selection of small drills
- A 4" engineer's square
- Task Lamp
- Pencils, pens and a small drawing board (if you have one)

- Long tape measure for surveying prototype buildings

If you need to solder up rainwater pipes and gutters you will also need the following:

- Soldering iron

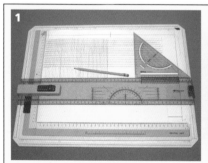

**1.** A small drawing board comes in handy when planning a building.

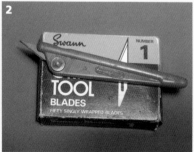

**2.** A typical inexpensive craft knife and a good supply of new blades.

**3.** A scraper board tool mounted on a pencil.
**4.** An engineer's square is very handy for

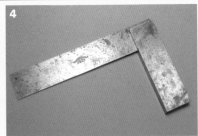

checking that the corners of buildings are at true right angles.

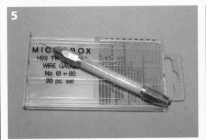

**5.** A set of small drills and a pin vice will enable you to fit door handles and open up

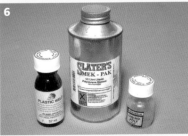
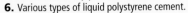

holes for rainwater pipes and the like.
**6.** Various types of liquid polystyrene cement.

**7.** Woodwork glue or white PVA adhesive is ideal for sticking wood, paper and card.

**8.** This white solvent-free adhesive is very useful for sticking plastic to card, plastic, metal or wood amongst other things.

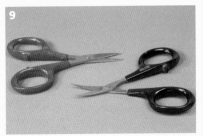

**9.** Straight and curved nail scissors for cutting thatch.

**10.** A selection of reasonable quality paint brushes.

**11.** Various matt enamel paints.

**12.** An inexpensive set of acrylic paints.

- Soldering iron stand (not essential but most useful)
- Flux or soldering fluid
- Solder

You are also likely to need the following to decorate or finish off your models:

- Aerosol car primer for metal parts
- A selection of reasonable quality small paint brushes for painting
- A wide selection of coloured matt enamels or acrylic paints
- White spirit/thinners for enamel paints

Finally the following glues and adhesives are worth keeping handy on the workbench:

- Liquid polystyrene cement
- PVA adhesive
- Impact adhesive
- Quick setting epoxy resin
- Superglue

Without wanting to sound too boring or repetitive, it is probably worth repeating that there are a number of quite serious heath and safety issues that, we as modellers, should be aware of before we get started:

- Always read the label of any glue, paint or solvent, they usually have clear instructions regarding their safe use and often tell you what to do if you accidentally misuse them.
- If a product recommends that they are used in a well-ventilated room, keep a window open and avoid breathing in fumes.
- If you can, look out for modern products that are solvent-free.
- Be careful with your craft knife, if you take your time and watch what you are doing, the occasional cut finger really can be avoided.
- Avoid splashes of spray paint in your eyes by wearing safety specs.
- Wear a mask to prevent spray being breathed in as well.
- If you have small children, always keep any pretty coloured pots and jars either well out of reach or locked away.
- Always supervise the junior model-maker when they are likely to be at risk.

The Fitzwilliam Arms, known locally as the Green Man, was my third scratch-built structure and incidentally my first attempt at thatching.

Many railway modellers, myself included, often want to make models of structures in the form that they were in a particular period in their history. During the course of my model making I have, on occasions, found it impossible to accurately survey a number of buildings that I really wanted to model as they were in the 1930s. Unfortunately, as is often the case with prototypes from days gone by, many structures may have either long since fallen into disrepair or have been completely demolished to make way for something new. If you are faced with a similar obstacle to me don't be put off, there are in fact a number of places you can start your search for records, photos and other invaluable historical information. Some of the better ones are;

• Specialist railway history societies
• Books – particularly on specialist railway topics and local history
• Postcard collections
• Museums
• Local history section of most libraries
• The internet
• Antiquarian booksellers and antiques fairs

• Old maps
• Old magazines
• If you can talk to people who lived or worked in or around your prototype's location while it was still in existence.
• Appeal to fellow enthusiasts for information – someone may already have all of the information you are looking for.

Perhaps the main disadvantage with detailed research of this kind is, as you might anticipate, that it can take a considerable period of time to uncover exactly what you are looking for. Sometimes you can find hoards of information purely by chance; I certainly did when I knocked on the door of the real life Well Cottage in Dogsthorpe. Although at first the owner was a little cautious, he soon agreed to let me walk around the perimeter of his property to take all of the photos that I wanted. Having by then established my genuine interest in the locality, he went inside and brought out his collection of old photos that revealed to me almost all of the cottages and old buildings in the area. It really was a model maker's dream come true, there was such a mine of information here that it has kept me going in modelling terms for years and

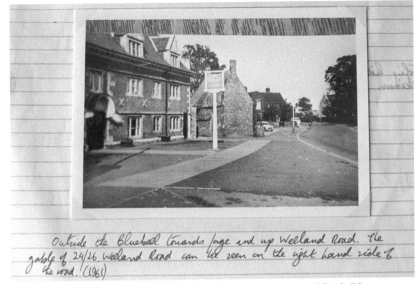

*Outside the Bluebell towards Page and up Welland Road. The gable of 24/26 Welland Road can be seen on the right hand side of the road! (1961)*

Old photos like this one in a scrap book can be invaluable when it comes to modelling buildings.

If you can, take as many photos like these as possible to show all aspects and construction details of the building you are planning to make.

The Green Man before being rethatched in a different style.

has left me with an array of long-term projects on the shelf for the future. The moral of this tale I suppose is not to be afraid to ask – you never know just what you will be able to find!

Although it may not immediately be obvious to the railway modeller there is a great wealth of information that can be gleaned from early large-scale maps. Being pretty accurately plotted they can usually be found and copied for a few pence at the local library and used to work out reasonably accurate proportions and dimensions that would otherwise be unobtainable. With updated versions of the same area often being available, revisions can also give us some pretty exacting details relating to changes in track layout, buildings on a particular site and of course the timeline of these changes made over a period of years.

If you are modelling a prototype that is still in existence you can of course, as I have already hinted, carry out a full survey with permission of its owner. If you have plenty of time this would normally involve measuring out and sketching of the whole of the structure. On the other hand, being inherently lazy, I do not usually bother with this rather laborious process; instead I rely on the proportions of the photographed elevations to the principal dimensions take on site. As you will soon see, this method saves a lot of time, is still surprisingly accurate and importantly avoids as much inconvenience as possible to the building occupier.

Although in the past I would have used a camera loaded with colour print film, I now thoroughly recommend the use of a decent digital camera to speed up the whole process. I invariably start by taking a square-on photograph of each of the building's elevations making sure that I stand centrally to the subject to avoid parallax or distortion of the resulting image. Wherever it is possible try to stand on something like a small stepladder to bring the camera in line with the centre of the subject and always use the equivalent of a 50mm standard lens rather than a wide angle one, again to reduce the effects of distortion. Next, largely as an *aide-memoire* during construction, I take as many detail shots of the building as I can, giving most attention to the pattern of any windows, doors, brick or stone bonding and any special features there might be. The next job is to set the scale by measuring the lengths of all of the main wall elevations and mark them neatly on a plan. Finally any distinctive features, door heights and window sizes can be measured, noted down and if necessary roughly sketched out while you are still on site.

Before the advent of digital technology, the only real way to draw up plans for your building was to get a set of large 7" x 5" or better still 8" x 6" photos, find some paper and some fine pens and set to converting your photos and site measurements using a scale rule and a calculator. Nowadays, with the aid of simple software, it is possible

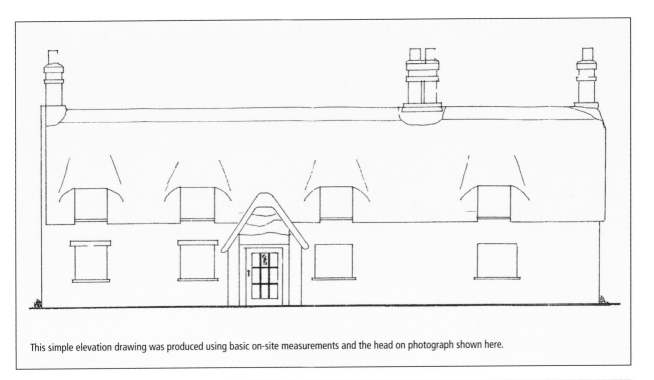

This simple elevation drawing was produced using basic on-site measurements and the head on photograph shown here.

to both convert the photographed elevations to scale and even draw them out on your PC. Being mindful that not all model-makers have access to these luxuries, and of course that most scale plans made from archive photos have to be made this way, I think it is worthwhile taking a look at the traditional drawn approach.

Before you start, it is worth remembering that the drawing that you make doesn't necessarily need to be a fully detailed architectural masterpiece, as its primary purpose is to give you a set of scale dimensions to work to, helping you visualise the model and plan the way you intend to construct it. So, if you haven't got a small drawing board, simply stick a piece of A3 paper down on a flat work surface with masking tape and you are ready to start

Firstly, draw a base line about 30mm above the bottom edge of the paper using an HB pencil and a straight edge. If your model is to have a stepped or sloping base it is worth at this stage, drawing in the approximate ground levels either above or below the base line. Next take the length of the wall as

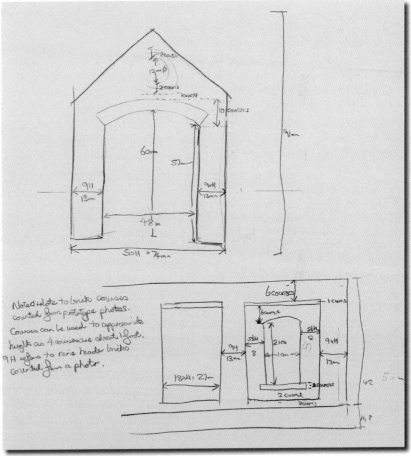

Notes made during the drawing of Shipston-on-Stour engine shed.

measured on site and convert it to scale which in my case is 1/76th or 4mm: 1'. If, for example, you have a wall that measures say 20' long simply multiply it by 4 to give a scale length of 80mm (ie: 4mm to 1'). In metric a measured length of 6090mm is divided by 76 to once again give the scale length of 80mm. Now plot this dimension on the base line of your drawing. Following this, draw in the vertical lines at the ends of the elevation.

Unless you have measured all of the dimensions during your site survey, the easiest method of ascertaining all other principal dimensions is to use a simple proportion factor based on a known measured dimension taken from the prototype to the corresponding dimension of a feature measured from the photographs. If you are not sure how this works follow this example:

If the scale length of a wall measured on site is 80mm (as calculated above) and the same wall shown in elevation on a photo measures 60mm, the proportion factor becomes 80/60 = 1.33 This means that all of the dimensions measured from the elevation photo can be multiplied by the factor of, in this instance, 1.33. So, if a door opening is 10mm wide on your head

on photo, it will need to be 13.3mm wide on the scale drawing.

In an effort to speed up the process, you can use the same factor to blow up the head on photo using a photocopier. Most modern machines have an enlarge/reduce facility so, as 1.33 is another way of writing a 33% enlargement, simply set the copy size to this setting and press the print button. Rather than trust my calculations I usually cross check the main dimension for accuracy and, if not exactly right, adjust the % increase/decrease setting by a percent at a time until it comes out exactly right. The resulting image will now be to scale and will allow you to simply transfer dimensions straight onto paper without further calculation or adjustment.

Irrespective of the way that you arrive at the correct dimension it is now time to add the tops of the walls, the eaves line and the roof and add any chimneys to the drawings. Finally transfer over all window and door positions and check that everything looks about right.

When the only information you can find are archive photos and the main plan dimensions are taken from old large-scale maps there are a a few tricks of the trade that you can use to enable

the same proportioning process to be used. You are admittedly limited by the details that you possess without the help of a site survey, but even when things are not pictured head-on, you can still make reasonably accurate assumptions about the missing measurements. Dimensions such as floor to ceiling heights average around 2.4m, with old cottages being somewhat smaller, and grander buildings, particularly those in the Victorian period, during which time many stations were built, somewhat larger. Similarly door heights can act as a good guide; industry standard single door openings are normally 2.1m high but can vary depending upon building use. Always gauge the height against any people in your picture; an educated guess will often be about right. Some common railway buildings are governed by a standard loading gauge so goods shed and engine shed door heights can be deduced pretty readily using the loading gauge as a guide.

In the absence of anything else, and particularly if you have the luxury of some decent clear photos, why not resort to counting bricks! As I am a chartered Quantity Surveyor, that's what some people think I do for a living, anyway - how wrong could they be! As most imperial bricks were

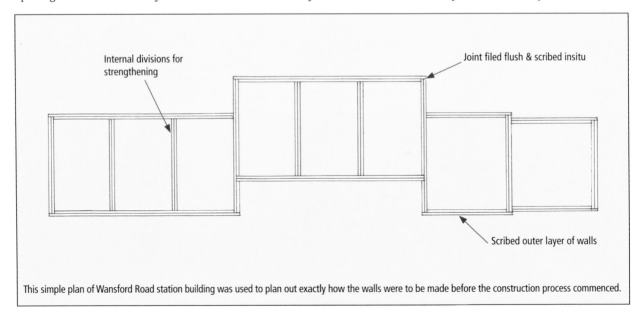

This simple plan of Wansford Road station building was used to plan out exactly how the walls were to be made before the construction process commenced.

made to a standard 225mm x 112.mm x 75mm module (including mortar joints) you can simply convert what you see on a photo to scale. I use a magnifying glass and a pointer to help the process and make very rough notes, just as the sample reproduced here. If, as your base, you have four horizontal brick courses to the foot; stretcher bricks (long ones on face) to be about 3mm to scale; header bricks (short ones on face) to be about 1.5mm to scale you won't go far wrong. I know this sounds particularly tedious but, believe me, is pretty accurate and is not half as bad to do in practice as it sounds. Always bear in mind that most period buildings were built in feet and inches. I wonder just how many times have I agonised over a proportioned dimension only to find that it works out to exactly 20' or another similar but precisely rounded off length. Components such as windows are commonly 4' or 5' high and have widths to the nearest foot or 6". Remember, without a precisely drawn architect's blueprint you will never be able to be totally accurate but, with a little thought and common sense you should be able to be somewhere fairly close.

Once you have completed all of the drawn elevations, I find it advisable to make a quick cross-section and draw out a plan that clearly shows the setting out of exactly how you intend to build the thickened walls in relation to one another. As you will see later in this book, I do not usually mitre the vertical joints between the walls, instead I prefer to make solid butt joints which are left to harden before they are filed flush will the surface of the wall. This means that the sheets of plastic can be made to overlap each other at the corners, so the way that they do so needs to be planned pretty much as shown on the accompanying sketch.

You can, if you feel inclined, add as much detail to your drawings as you

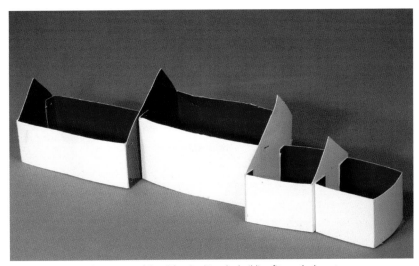

This simple card mock-up is a useful tool for checking the building fits on the layout.

want. I don't normally bother at this stage, partly as I think the drawing needs to be a simple way of producing the dimensional information that is needed, but mainly as I am far too impatient and just can't wait to get on with the model.

If, like me, you now have a digital camera, or indeed can scan in old photos, you can quickly resize and print out these images on your home printer. Indeed, once checked for scale you can even use these instead of drawings. Being a little too cluttered with all of the prototype's detail I still prefer to use them to make a simple outline sketch to start with but use them later when fine detailing is added to the model.

Even if you want to build a freelance structure to fit a particular sized gap on your layout, planning still is just as important but is much simpler to do. Always start with a plan indicating the exact space available and work from there. Once again follow the basic drawing techniques and check that it does fit the available space before you start building. If you do not know too much about typical building construction technology and standard dimensions it is always a good idea, I reckon, to base your model loosely on something that you have seen whether on you travels or in a book. If you can,

try to approximate floor to ceiling heights and sizes of windows and doors from similar types of buildings as much as possible to ensure authenticity, otherwise simply sketch out the elevations just the same as we have seen above.

Now that you have spent several hours surveying and planning your model I think that it is well-worth an extra half an hour or so to check that it will fit neatly into its intended location on your layout. To do this you can quickly make a simple, no frills, full-size mock up or template from scraps of old card. If you start by marking out all of the adjacent walls to scale it is a quick and easy task to cut out the pieces, fold the corners, and glue or staple the mock-up together. If it is possible I prefer to leave fixing tabs, just like you would find in a card kit, to aid assembly and rarely bother with adding a roof. Seeing the card template in place, even in its rough and ready form, really can boost your enthusiasm for the project in hand, this one certainly spurred me on to get my tools out and get started straight away.

Having now taken the time and trouble to plan out your project, it is perhaps timely to take a look through some of the common elements of building construction.

# BRICKWORK

Shipston-on-Stour engine shed is typical of many lineside structures built in brick, but with many decorative features.

Before describing the materials I usually recommend to make brick walls, it is well worth taking a technology time out for a quick look at the standard size of bricks and some of the types of brickwork bonds that are widely found.

## Common Types Of Brickwork

Today most bricks come as units that measure 215mm long x 102.5mm wide x 65mm high. With a mortar joint on each side this results in a 225mm x 75mm unit on face. For 4mm modellers, 3mm x 1mm bricks are about the right size to represent the pre-metrication standard of four brick courses to the foot. To ensure the strength and stability necessary in the walls that they build into, bricks are laid to a bond that usually ensures that the vertical joints between adjoining bricks are not in line in neighbouring rows. Bonds comprise bricks that are laid lengthways in the wall known as Stretchers and bricks laid across the wall called Headers. There are two main bonds that are commonly found on railway buildings, these are English Bond and Flemish Bond. As you can see from the photos and drawings English Bond features alternate courses of headers and stretchers whereas Flemish Bond comprises alternate bricks laid as stretchers and headers. Both of these bonds result in walls that are one brick thick and reasonably decorative.

**1.** English Bond in yellow bricks adjacent to the ex GNR main line.

**2.** Flemish Bond found on a between the wars semi.

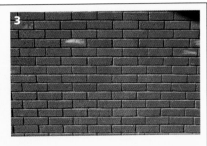

**3.** Stretcher Bond typical of modern cavity wall construction.

**4.** Always look out for variations, this example has three courses of stretchers that are tied together every fourth course by headers.

**5.** Herringbone brickwork used as an infill to a timber frame.

**6.** A typical combination of brickwork used with stone quoins.

Generally speaking most common types of railway and domestic buildings (up to three storeys high) have walls of this thickness. Larger goods sheds and multi storey warehouses would have thicker walls particularly on the lower levels.

A third bond, Stretcher bond, is also widely found. Here all bricks are stretchers so the wall width is just half a brick thick. These narrower walls are more suitable for small, lightly loaded structures such as huts and outbuildings and, since the widespread introduction of cavity wall construction in around the 1930's, as the outer skin of more modern buildings. Over the years I have all too often seen good models ruined by the inappropriate use of stretcher bond in their external walls. Perhaps this is because we all draw walls like this in primary school and have little knowledge of when either English or Flemish bonds should have been used instead.

Having briefly mentioned cavity walls above, it is worth noting that these usually have a brick outer skin tied to

an inner skin of concrete blocks with metal fixings, not surprisingly called ties. From the modeller's point of view you only see the outer surface so the bond is all that is important here.

## Modelling Brickwork

In addition to various makes of printed brickpaper and card on the market there are several types of ready-embossed brickwork available to the model-maker. The most popular are probably Slater's, of 'Plastikard' fame, who cater for the popular scales and Wills, who produce sheets for the 4mm scratch-builder. Most makes of brickwork are usually available in English, Flemish and Stretcher bonds.

It is of course possible to individually scribe bricks onto plain sheets of plastic card in exactly the same manner as we will use for stonework. Having experimented with this painstaking process on several occasions however, I would only recommend its use for very small areas such as an infilled door opening on a stone wall or brick facings to

jambs and quoins. Large areas can of course be covered but to my mind never really seem to look as uniform and neat as the embossed brick varieties that are available.

Another method used by some modellers is to use old-fashioned computer chads to represent bricks. This, as you might anticipate, is a pretty time consuming process with each brick needing to be individually painted and positioned on the wall. Using the four courses to a foot pointer I find most of these to be a bit over scale in 4mm and rarely feature the header bricks used in most of our common types of brickwork.

The type of embossed brick you use is really down to preference. I find the thicker Wills panels to be ideal for some jobs such as garden walls; largely as two strips glued back to back result in a reasonable scale thickness. Standard sheets are about 65 thou thick and measure 133mm x 76 mm. This factor does, I feel, limit its use to all but the smaller buildings where I find it is very quick and easy to use as no backing or

**1.** Materials available from left to right: Slater's Stretcher Bond, Slater's Flemish Bond, Slater's English Bond, Wills' English Bond.

**2.** This blocked up door opening and its brick surround has brickwork scribed by hand.

strengthening layer is normally required. Having noted this, the inexperienced modeller should bear in mind that these rather thick sheets are much harder to cut neatly with the average modelling knife than ordinary plastic card. Similarly the mitred joints that are necessary are a bit more time consuming to get right and decorative brick features, for example flush soldier courses and bands, such as those forming brick lintels and arches above windows, cannot be easily inlaid. On larger areas of walling I find that neat seamless joints between abutting sheets are very difficult to make. The only practical way to get around this problem is to hide them behind rainwater pipes, piers or the like. If you want to see these sheets in use, my first *BRM* book *Lineside Buildings* features stage-by-stage construction of one of the Wills 'Craftsman' range of building kits. Unlike most other types of kit, these use standard embossed sheets that, just like scratch-building, need to be marked out, cut to size and assembled.

## Making Brick Walls

Having tried various methods over the years, I still prefer the thinner 20 thou thick Slater's product which, despite one or two tales from old modellers about the regularity of its coursing, find much

more easy to cut and adapt, especially when used as a facing to a thicker wall. Indeed, as you will see shortly, I always use the brick sheet as the outer skin of a laminated wall with two thicknesses of plain 40 thou sheet behind and a sturdy supporting structure to form the shell. Where brick detailing is flush with the face of the wall, such as brick arches, these can be inlaid into cut outs in the brick facing using plain sheet of the same overall thickness and size. Once dry, the decorative brickwork is simply scribed on with a scraperboard tool. Similarly projecting bands or corbels can be built up by adding one or more additional layers to the face of the embossed sheet.

Having, over the years, experimented with varying thicknesses of plastic card backing, I have adopted the two-layer method largely for the following reasons.
• Firstly, left unbacked the plastic sheet is likely to warp and twist due to the effects of the solvent.
• If you use two layers of differing thickness the plastic has a tendency to pull and curl towards the thinner layer.
• 40 thou sheet just happens to be about the right scale thickness for window and door reveals in 4mm scale.

Although you can mitre the joints between walls, I rarely do. Instead I butt joint the layers of 40 thou sheet together making allowance for the embossed layer at each corner. When

This is what can happen to a wall made from two different thicknesses of plastic card.

the joint has been set aside to harden thoroughly I simply cut or scribe back the missing courses and smooth over the surface. In making any wall, it is particularly important to get the configuration of the layers right to achieve the corner detail illustrated. If in doubt, sketch it out! You will certainly be more likely to overcome any possible mistakes that would show up when you come to assemble your model later.

As brickwork can vary significantly in complexity from building to building, it is probably best to firstly consider a very straightforward plain brick faced wall before we move on to something a little more difficult and ornate in the shape of Shipston-on-Stour engine shed. Finally we shall see how a more complicated wall can be made in the shape of the front wall of a former Methodist Chapel.

## Simple Walls

Starting with the simplest of walls, the first stage is to take a sheet of embossed facing bricks and mark out the wall. Next cut out the wall and remove the window and door apertures. If you look at the first photo you will see that the lintel positions are now pencilled in above the openings. Before you carefully cut these out take a sheet of 40thou plastic card and place it behind the wall. Using the partly cut out wall as a template neatly mark out the wall on the plain sheet. You can, if necessary at this stage drill a few holes in the plain plastic sheet to enable the solvent to be introduced into the joint between this and the embossed layer. Now slide the brick sheet with the lintel positions cut out over the pencil marked plain layer such that the apertures line up and the wall perimeters match. If everything is perfectly aligned, tack weld the two layers together with a spot or two of solvent. A quick check to see that the two parts have not slipped and the rest of the solvent holding the two walls together can be applied.

The next stage is to cut out 'concrete' lintels from plain 20thou plastic card, such that they are a nice tight fit in the apertures above the openings and that the bottom edge lines up with the pencil mark on the underlying layer of the wall. Once these have been stuck in place and have been given a chance to harden, it is a fairly simple task to cut out the windows and doors from the first backing sheet using the embossed layer as a template and a guide, making sure as you do so, that the knife doesn't dig in to the upper layer as it cuts out the one underneath.

My preferred method of making, and indeed strengthening, pretty much any structure revolves around the same basic two-ply lamination made from 40thou plastic card. Having one layer of embossed bricks and a single layer of 40thou sheet at the moment, the next stage, yes you've guessed, is to mark out a second backing layer of 40thou plastic card with apertures larger than the openings. These need to be slightly larger all round, so that when fitted together rebates are formed to take the windows and doors. When this has been stuck in place behind the first two layers the completed basic wall assembly can be

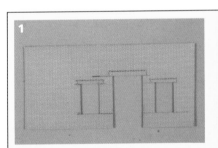

**1.** The embossed brick layer to the boiler house is marked and cut out.

**2.** A backing layer of 40 thou plastic card is marked out using the brick wall as a template.

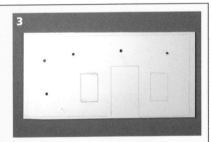

**3.** Holes drilled to allow solvent to be introduced between the sheets.

**4.** A third thickness is prepared to stiffen up the walls.

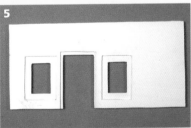

**5.** This layer is fixed behind to leave rebates for the windows and doors.

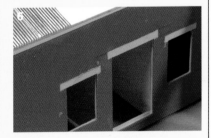

**6.** The lintels can clearly be seen in this front view of the wall.

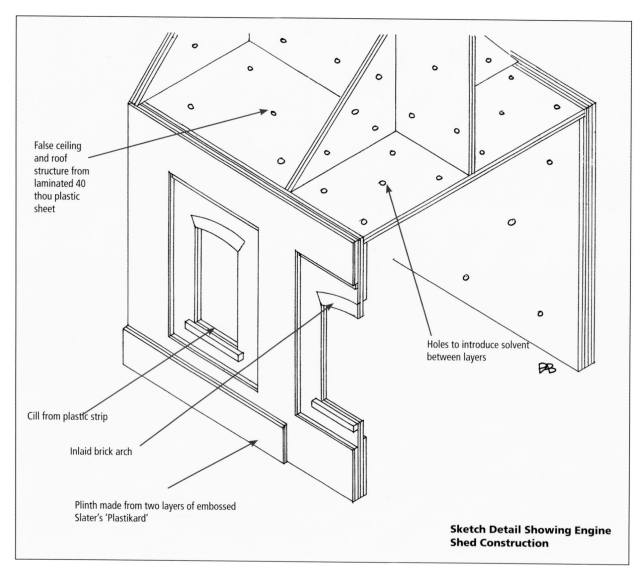

False ceiling and roof structure from laminated 40 thou plastic sheet

Holes to introduce solvent between layers

Cill from plastic strip

Inlaid brick arch

Plinth made from two layers of embossed Slater's 'Plastikard'

**Sketch Detail Showing Engine Shed Construction**

put aside to harden (you can, if you wish, load the flat wall with books or something heavy to keep it flat) and the basic wall is complete.

## Brick Detailing

Moving on, Shipston-on-Stour engine shed is a little more complicated. Perhaps the best place to start is to take a good look at the accompanying sketches and photographs. As you can see, the engine shed's walls can be constructed from a sandwich of varying thicknesses of both plain and embossed plastic card.

To make walls like this, start by taking a sheet of Slater's embossed English Bond brickwork and mark out all of the window positions together with the tops of the curves to the brick arches at the head of each opening. To mark and neatly trim the arc I find that a sharp scriber held firmly in a pair of ordinary compasses will soon do both jobs. A few light scores will readily mark the arc whereas, if you apply a bit more pressure, the plastic will be scored right through and can be snapped away leaving a nice clean cut. Straight lines on the other hand are, as always, best achieved using a sharp craft knife and a steel ruler.

Having cut out the brick-facing sheet it can now be bonded to a backing sheet of 40thou plastic card.

At this stage the brick arches can be made in a similar way to the concrete lintels seen previously. Being arched with a brickwork face, these cannot be made from off-the-peg embossed plastic sheet. The best way of making them, I find, is once again using the compass/scriber method, cutting them from plain plastic sheet of a matching thickness to that of the brickwork. As you can guess, these pieces do need to fit perfectly into the curves already cut out on the walls so that they can be inlaid, marquetry-fashion, in place. To ensure a really good, tight fit you might find it necessary to clean up the edges with the touch of a small file prior to final fitting, but otherwise these parts are simple to make and glue into position. When the solvent has had a chance to harden, the next task is to scribe the individual bricks onto the face of the plastic card *in situ* using a scraperboard marker tool. Finally remove the window apertures using the facing sheet as a guide for the knife to follow. If you are worried about the knife cutting into the side of the opening you can, if you prefer, always use a steel edge.

To end up with the decorative but structural brick facework of the prototype, it is necessary to take another sheet of embossed plastic sheet and make up some external overlays. In order to give the correct appearance of depth, these will again need to be bonded to a backing layer of 40 thou plastic card. Once these have been cut out in turn and trimmed to size they can be simply bonded to the front of the wall ensuring, in so doing, that the brick bond is matched to and in line with that on the rest of

the wall. As we want to give the model strength and reduce the potential risk of warping (largely as there isn't a base or floor to keep things nice and true in this structure), we can add yet another layer of 40 thou plastic card to the back face of the wall. This layer has a secondary function as its over-sized window cut outs also form recesses for the windows. In addition the brick window reveals are kept to as prototypical depth as possible.

Finally, to complete the wall, various adornments such as corbelled

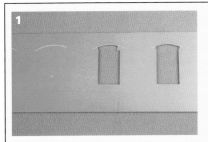

**1.** The windows are cut out from a sheet of embossed plastic card.

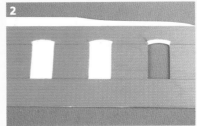

**2.** With a thickening sheet added, the curved brick details to the window heads are added.

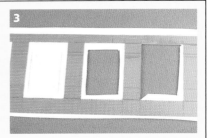

**3.** Outer layers of the sandwich wall construction are made up separately.

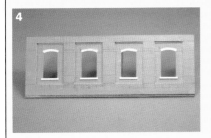

**4.** Once brought together corbels and cills are added.

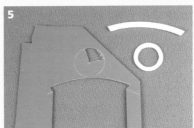

**5.** End wall components showing the scribed method of cutting out curved plastic edges.

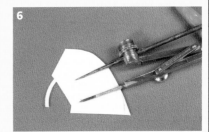

**6.** A simple scriber held in a pair of compasses is the tool for making consistent curves.

**7.** Taken a stage further the end wall takes shape.

**8.** Seen from behind, the wall shows the rebate for the windows and the holes that allow plastic solvent to pass between the sandwiched layers.

brickwork can be added from scraps of embossed sheet and the window cills can be made from plastic strip cut to size. As some form of detailing or another is found on most brick walls, here is a quick summary of the most common features:

**Plinths** are thickenings found usually surrounding the base of the walls of many old buildings. These commonly have a one third brick projection (or a multiple of this) and in many cases feature a sloping or weathered top. To make these I usually cut out a strip of embossed brickwork one course wider than the actual face of the plinth and carefully file the top brick course away until a neat sloping top edge with a consistent profile results. Once prepared the strip (or strips) is attached to the perimeter of the building using solvent as normal.

**Corbelling** is where subsequent courses of bricks are set slightly overhanging the course below it. Often seen as decorative bands on external walls and chimney stacks, corbelling is very easy to replicate in model form by overlaying single

Close up of the complete wall.

thickness strips of embossed bricks on top of each other. In reality the overhang is no more than one third of a brick width deep per course so the 20 thou thick plastic strips are about right for scale.

**Projecting horizontal and vertical brick bands** can also be made from strips of the same materials with, in some cases, the addition of small lengths of Microstrip to represent projecting feature band courses and the like.

**Cills** often comprise a row of bricks to contrast that of the wall. They can also comprise one or two rows of corbelled brick course traditionally capped with either plain tiles or slates. Without going into too much detail these are easily modelled using a combination of Microstrip and embossed plastic card components.

**Special bricks** are usually specially moulded with ornate decorations, some such as cant bricks have simple sloping surfaces that can be easy modelled using a file and scriber.

**Brick arches,** as we have already seen can be either flat or curved in pattern and take the place of a stone or concrete lintel at the window head.

**Stone embellishments** are very often incorporated in brick walls particularly those on grand or important buildings. These can be modelled in much the same way as you will see in the stonework section.

**1.** A simple brick window cill from Wells on the GER.

**2.** Note the GNR end detail on Little Bytham's cills.

**3.** Toddington on the GWR has a flush variant.

**4.** This tiled cill is more common in a domestic situaton.

**1.** A modern head detail with both cant bricks and soldier course.

**2.** This MR lintol from Rushden has a decorative botton edge.

**3.** A three course brick arch is found on the GNR building at Little Bytham.

**4.** Gauged *voussoirs* forming an arch at Wells Next The Sea.

**5.** These special bricks form an arch at Toddington on the GWR.

**6.** A typical Georgian embellished window-head on a brick wall.

This brick built engine shed features a plywood frame as an alternative to laminated plastic card.

## Ornate Brickwork

As you can see from the front elevation of the Methodist chapel, brickwork can be very complicated indeed and comprises almost all of the decorative features noted above. In reality the way it was made is far from complicated using some of the simple methods already described.

Basically, modelling the embossed wall, window apertures and first layer of backing are all pretty much standard. The curved arch, although a little more difficult to make than the engine shed, relies on exactly the same inlaying process as we used there, but needs a little more precision compass work in its marking out. Once again, the curved inlay is marked out using compasses with a scriber fitted to score the edge of the curve and the individual bricks are

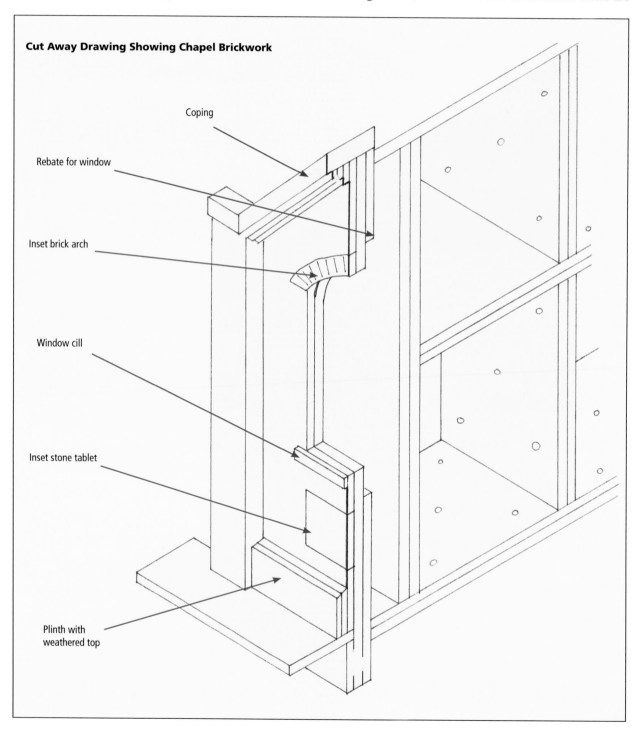

**Cut Away Drawing Showing Chapel Brickwork**

Coping

Rebate for window

Inset brick arch

Window cill

Inset stone tablet

Plinth with weathered top

scribed on with a scraperboard tool. By making a series of cuts fanning out from the waste edge of the scribed line on both the inside and outside edges of the arch inlay, you will be able to neatly remove the excess plastic right up to the line of the curve without too much trouble at all.

If you look at the brick arch above the entrance door, you will see that it is not a true curve and has a flatter top. Although it is made using the same basic technique you do need to take a lot more care in ensuring that the cut out in the embossed layer is an exact match.

In conclusion, I would always suggest that any model-maker should take a detailed look at the prototype to be reproduced in miniature and pick the material that suits him best for the purpose. Don't forget to take loads of photos if you can and watch out for extensions to buildings, as these can frequently be built in a different bond and style to the original structure.

The prototype Methodist chapel is now in use as a scout hut.

Typical of many small chapels, this ornate example is seen on the author's Paston Ridings layout.

A Pannier tank simmers gently outside Shipston-on-Stour shed.

Another of the Shipston-on-Stour buildings is this small engine shed, a building type typical of many branch lines throughout the country. Ideally suited for modelling in plastic card, this interesting little structure makes a super candidate to reveal its construction processes in the Prototype Project section of this book.

## Walls and Assembly

Perhaps the best place to start this feature is to take a good look at the accompanying photographs. As you have already seen in the chapter on brickwork, the engine shed's walls can be constructed from a sandwich of varying thicknesses of both plain and embossed plastic card.

Once again, the basic assembly strategy starts, much the same as any building, with the four walls. To this a sub-roof, longitudinal brace under the ridge line and some triangular shaped roof supports are added. Take a quick look at the drawing on page 20 and all, I hope, will become clear.

## Windows

When you are modelling a specific prototype such as this, you really do need to make sure that the windows you use are a good match, both in size and architectural appearance. Once again I couldn't find brass window etchings that were exactly right for the job but, having uncovered a few possible candidates in my drawer, I eventually decided to use some of the excellent industrial windows produced by Dan Pinnock of D&S.

As with the goods shed, the pane size

The derelict engine shed as it was in the late 1980s (The late Michael Warner).

was just about right, but these windows actually had five panes vertically and four panes horizontally, whereas the ones I wanted were only four panes high and three panes wide. This meant that modification was necessary, I had to very carefully snip away the surplus panes from the etchings and just as carefully file up the cut edges ready for fabrication. Just as with the goods shed, I cut a length of spare brass sprue from the etching that was slightly longer than the height of the finished window and soldered it along the long edge of the modified window. Similarly another piece of scrap was added to the shorter edge. A quick tidy up with the file and all eight windows were ready for fixing to the plastic structure using Evo Stik's solvent free contact adhesive.

## Doors and Roof Ventilators

The engine shed's large timber doors were, in effect, very easy to construct. In fact they consist of 40thou thick pieces of plastic card cut to size with the planking scribed on both sides using a scraperboard tool. Care had to be taken while scribing the curves to the top edge and the curved timber members that fit into the opening, but otherwise no real problems were encountered. To make the large timbers that brace the rear of each door, I took lengths of rectangular

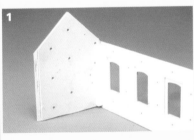

**1.** Assembly begins with the first corner stuck and strengthened.

**2.** Four walls attached – the building takes shape.

**3.** A false ceiling, longitudinal brace and roof supports are then added.

**4.** Close up of the corner detail.

The completed model.

## Roof and Rainwater Goods

The roof slopes, as you've already guessed, comprise once again two layers of 40 thou plastic card. In this instance, I cut the backing layer slightly smaller than the actual roof itself to form a rebate, that fitted snugly inside the walls, so that only one thickness was visible at the edges. As the roof vents were already in place, the only other tricky task was to make certain that the cut outs were in the correct positions along the ridge using the measure, check, cut and fit method. If you are in any doubt whatsoever, always cut the holes out slightly smaller than they should be and then carefully trim or file the plastic card until it is a perfect fit.

To replicate the slate covering, I opted to use cut strips of artist's watercolour paper bonded to the roof slopes in layers and used brass section for the gutters and down pipes. For a full description of both of these elements see the slate roofing and rainwater goods sections of this book respectively.

plastic section from the Evergreen range, trimmed them to size and simply solvent welded them in place on the inner face of the door.

Once again the roof ventilators were a pretty straightforward exercise in plastic card modelling. The illustration shows

the various stages of construction from the basic assembly on the left to the completed ventilator on the right. When all of these had been constructed, they were fixed in place along the spine of the roof support structure, such that they were both vertical and correctly spaced.

**1.** Various stage of roof vent assembly.

**2.** The roof vents are fixed into slots cut along the inner ridge.

**3.** Plastic roof slopes are added.

**4.** Strips of pre-cut watercolour paper make up the roofing slates.

**5.** Close up of the finished roof prior to painting.

**6.** Gutters and rainwater pipes are made up from brass section.

## Painting

Arguably this was the most tricky and time-consuming element of the whole building process. Thanks mainly to the prototype being built in alternate courses of red and blue engineering bricks, I had the monumental task of replicating the striped effect in 1mm wide bands horizontally across the whole of the engine shed. Furthermore, careful study of the photos revealed that the coloured bands didn't follow directly around the corners onto the adjacent wall. Instead they were staggered, such that the same course would be blue on the sides and red on the ends and *vice versa*.

Now I know I had already painted the thin brick plinths on Shipston's goods shed, but to paint something as complicated as this bothered me quite a lot. As I am sure you will agree, a bad paint job can ruin a half-decent model where crooked courses would end up looking totally ridiculous. Well, having messed around on a few scraps of embossed plastic card, I eventually took 'the bull by the horns' as they say and got stuck in!

Firstly I mixed some Precision/Phoenix Paint's matt Dark Brick Red (P953) with a touch of matt orange/terracotta and a spot of brown and effectively painted all of the walls a red brindled colour. Having let this dry thoroughly for a day or two, I started to very carefully add some of the contrasting bands using Precision/Phoenix Engineer's Blue Brick (P954). Even with the embossed lines to follow I found that it was almost impossible to keep the bands totally straight and basically ended up with the first bay looking very stripy and not at all as I intended.

The problem was in effect two fold. Firstly the blue was a bit overpowering and needed toning down a little and secondly the edges of the blue bands were, in places, running into the mortar joints. Once again I turned to some scrap plastic and after a bit more experimentation came up with a very simple solution indeed. Just as you can use a grey wash to run into a contrasting mortar in brick joints, I applied a thin wash of the Dark Brick Red (P953) over all of the walls. The results were very pleasing, the mortar joints were now a matching colour, the courses were straight and the thin wash of colour had just toned down the blue courses enough to make them look much more realistic.

Now all I had to do was repeat the process on the other seven bays and a couple of ends as well! Ok, so I have to admit this wasn't my favourite painting job, I did it a bay or so at a time, I even went away on holiday to avoid it, only to find some still waiting for me on my return. The moral I suppose is don't be put off completely, do a bit from time to time when you are in the mood, set it aside when you are not and eventually the job will be done.

With the walls painted, the rest was a lot easier. I used some Humbrol matt grey for the slate roofing, Revell matt brown (M84) for the rainwater goods, to match other buildings on the layout, and finished things off with Precision/Phoenix GWR Stone No.1 (P21) elsewhere.

## Conclusion

Despite the problem with painting and the complication of having to inlay the brick arches, I really enjoyed making this neat little engine shed. Ok, so there were a few awkward bits to sort out along the way, but these, I reckon, are all part of the fun. Without a bit of experimentation and improvisation we certainly wouldn't learn new skills and techniques and our fascinating hobby wouldn't be, in my opinion, half as interesting and rich.

Out of use as an engine shed but still in good condition (The late Michael Warner Collection).

# STONEWORK

The stonework on this model of the GNR Wansford Road station building has been individually scribed by using a scraper board tool on ordinary sheets of plastic card.

When I first started to model stone structures I didn't really give a second thought to the technicalities of stone wall construction, but it wasn't long before I became aware that there are, in fact, a host of stone wall types, ranging from the neatly faced varieties commonly found on grand designs such as stately homes, Victorian civic buildings and banks, to the rustic nature of the roughly hewn stone blocks used widely in many regions. The same architectural array can indeed be found in the stone buildings that we can see from the train, many of which pre-dated our railways by a few hundred years or so. With so many regional colour variations, stone sizes and use limitations caused by certain strata, it is probably a good time to get out the textbooks and take a closer look at the basic types before exploring some of the ways in which we can best model the various styles and patterns of stonework that we often encounter.

## Common Types Of Stonework

Although it may not be evident to the lay-modeller there are, broadly speaking, two principal types of stone walling. These are known in the trade as 'Rubble' and 'Ashlar'.

'Rubble' walls, as the name suggests, are built from stones that come to site pretty much as they have been quarried.

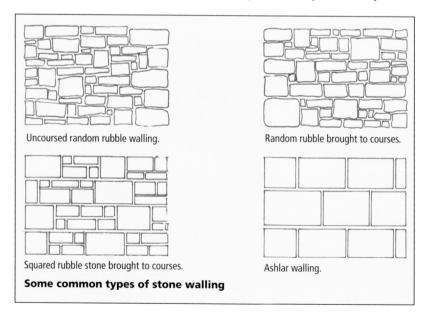

Uncoursed random rubble walling.

Random rubble brought to courses.

Squared rubble stone brought to courses.

Ashlar walling.

**Some common types of stone walling**

The simplest forms of these are termed random uncoursed rubble walls and random rubble brought to courses. In both instances the stones surrounding window and door openings are normally dressed to result in tidy perpendicular apertures.

Depending on the area of the country and its local type of stone, some rubble walls comprise blocks of stone that have been roughly squared off before laying to give a slightly better appearance. These are known as squared rubble walls and fall into four types - uncoursed squared rubble, squared rubble brought to courses, regular coursed rubble and the strangely termed snecked rubble.

From the modeller's point of view the only real difference is in the way that the pattern of all of the stones are set out (so take careful note of the prototype and copy exactly what you can see). It is also worth noting that walls that are brought to courses are in practice much quicker to replicate on a model, largely as a lot of the horizontal joints can be marked and scribed using a steel straight edge as a guide whereas random varieties have to be infilled freehand.

'Ashlar' walling on the other hand comprise stones that have been squarely cut and dressed to result in walls with extremely fine joints and a very neat appearance. As you might

guess such a labour intensive treatment would be pretty expensive, so prototypes built in this way would be limited to the more stately and important of structures such as vicarages and manors in the countryside and banks and other high profile buildings in towns and cities. In most instances the exposed face of the stone is either given a smooth or decorative tooled finish. When modelling an ashlar structure, have a careful look around the prototype and be careful not to fall into a potential trap. Quite often, largely due to the high construction costs already noted, what appears to have been built completely of faced stonework has in

**1.** Coursed rubble stonework.

**2.** More coursed rubble stonework – note the variation in stone sizes in this example.

**3.** A complete mixture of well weathered rubble and ashlar stonework.

**4.** Coursed rubble generally to courses but what has happened in the middle?

**5.** Alternate bands of rough rubble and ashlar stones.

**6.** Squared rubble walling.

**7.** This rubble wall has been raised using a mixture of flints and bricks.

**8.** Uncoursed rubble walling with raised pointing.

**9.** Ashlar bands with neat squared rubble infilling between them.

**10** Ashlar quoins and banding to squared rubble walling.

**11.** Ashlar stonework with course joints and a simple tooled finish.

**12.** Regular ashlar stonework with fine joints.

fact been cheapened by building the back or less prominent elevations in either brickwork or rubble stone.

## Modelling Stonework

I always feel, from the model maker's perspective, that it is very important to capture the feel, texture and style of each individual prototype. To help achieve this I usually take a number of close-up photographs before I begin showing the general pattern of the stonework and supplement this with as many detailed shots of specific features as I can. The accompanying examples illustrate just a few of the different styles and variations that can be found if you look closely.

Now that we have a basic insight into the construction technology for most common types of stonework, it is time to have a quick look at some of the popular ways we can reproduce them

in model form. Looking around our local model shop we will find that there are several sorts of sheet stonework available off the shelf and pretty much ready to use. They are:
• Pre-coloured printed 'brick and stone papers'. As the name suggests these are flat sheets that are very quick and easy to use provided you are happy to stick them onto a fairly substantial card or balsa base. Being printed, this type of stonework has no relief or texture to the surface but, if care is taken, can actually give some pretty convincing results.
• Embossed card sheets. These are, I feel, a step up from the paper variety. Although they are much thicker and, if I am honest, a bit harder to cut, these have the combined benefit of being pre-coloured with a much more realistic textured face.
• Embossed or injection moulded

polystyrene stonework. These are widely available from the likes of Slater's and Wills. If you haven't seen them, Slater's sheets are about 20thou thick and measure roughly 300mm x 190mm in size. They are pretty uniform in pattern and come in a variety of colours. Wills pre-coloured sheets are smaller and thicker being 132mm x 75mm x 60 thou thick and the joints are noticeably deeper than the Slater's alternative. From the modeller's point of view both can be used to make realistic reproductions of stone structures, but need a little more skill to use, particularly where sheets have to be joined, and really need to be painted to convincingly match the colour variation of any prototype.

The main disadvantage of all manufactured sheets, whether card or plastic, is that it is very difficult for the model-maker to faithfully reproduce

This stone cottage and barn features scribed stonework and is based on a prototype from Elton in Cambridgeshire.

the special stones that almost always exist around the windows, doors and at the corners of most stone structures. Many modellers chose to reproduce these stones in time-honoured tradition by overlaying them in front of the main layer. Ok, so the result may not be prototypically flush with the face of the building, but if made from thin enough material, shouldn't look too bad at all. In an attempt to overcome this problem many modellers, me included, choose to scratch-build stonework by scribing the individual stones onto a suitable backing sheet. There are two common materials used for this, they are:

• Plain plastic card
• Plaster or clay facing to a card or wooden structure

Having tried both of the above I must readily admit a preference to scribing stonework directly onto plastic card using a scraperboard tool, largely as I feel that fine detail can be reproduced much better in this way. The clay is great for some of the coarser types of stone and really comes into its own in the larger scales, particularly where you need to model a rough textured finish to the walls.

Before we move on there are a couple of other methods used to reproduce stonework that should be considered for the record. They are:

• Cutting out individual plastic card stones and sticking them one by one on a plain plastic shell. I have seen this done once and have never felt the need to try this very time consuming method for myself!
• Real stone. Although mainly confined to modellers of Welsh narrow gauge in the larger scales, shale can be used to model some very realistic state walling indeed. Have a look at Peter Kazer's book on the topic and you will see just what I mean.

Now that we have considered the alternatives, the best way to see exactly what goes on during the construction process is to take a closer look at my

preferred method to make a scribed stone wall from start to finish.

## Making Scribed Stone Walls

The basic element forming the external walls of near enough all of my plastic card buildings is the two layers of 40 thou plastic card that are bonded together using a solvent adhesive such as 'Mek Pak'. Once framed together with adequate bracing and supports, you end up with a surprisingly strong structure. Typically the sequence of events for making walls is:

• Setting out
• Scribing
• Adding windows surrounds/features
• Backing/strengthening.

## Setting Out

Having already roughly planned the way you want your model to be built

and how that walls are to be joined to each other, it is time to start setting the model out on a sheet, or rather sheets, of plastic card. Unless you are limited by the length of the plastic sheet, I find it best to try, wherever possible, to get as many adjoining elevations next to each other. This will not only enable the stone courses and bonding to be carried around corners with a perfect match, but will also make scribing a lot simpler.

Starting with a fresh sheet of 40 thou plastic card, trim the long edge using a sharp craft knife and a steel rule. This will ensure an accurate square foundation for the whole setting out process. Then, with the aid of a small engineer's square, pencil in the vertical lines at the ends of all walls. Following this, draw a line 10mm above and parallel to the bottom edge of the plastic sheet. This margin will allow

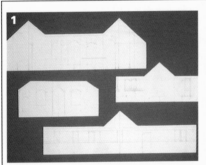

**1.** Each wing of the building is marked out on a sheet of plastic card and the basic shapes are cut out slightly oversize so that they can be trimmed down to the exact sizes once scribed.

**2.** The individual wings are trimmed to size.

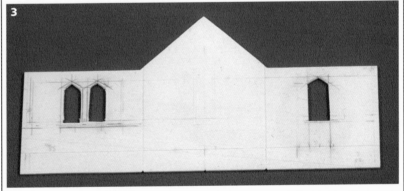

**3.** With the windows marked out the apertures are firstly roughed out before the exact lines are finally cut out.

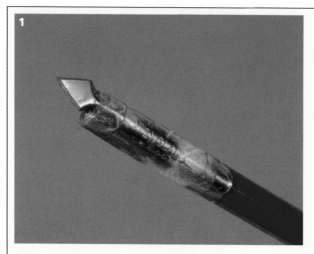

**1.** A scraper board tool is used to scribe stonework.

**2.** Stonework detail is added using the scraper board tool.

you to fix the completed building into the scenery at a later stage (if your model is on a sloping site this line should be drawn to reflect the contours all around the building). Next measure out and add the remaining outlines of all the walls detailing the basic window and door apertures.

At this stage I would suggest that you double check, with reference to your photographs and drawings, that all of the pencil lines are in the correct positions and that the doors and windows are in roughly the correct proportions and relationship with each other. If you are happy, then scribe along all the pencil lines in turn to prevent them being rubbed off by a sweaty hand as the rest of the detail is added.

We can now move on to adding the feature stonework. To do this, start by pencilling in the quoin stones (the larger ones at the corners) and the jambs (either side of the windows and doors). Once again check that you are happy with their positions, take another close look at the photos if you need to, and then scribe them in. Following this, repeat the process with all of the larger more distinctive stones, taking great care to carry the bond around the angles and capture the style and individual character of the prototype as you do so.

## Scribing

Scribing itself is a surprisingly quick and easy process. The knack, if you can call it a knack, is to hold the scraper board tool pretty much in the same way as you would a pen but in so doing maintaining the diamond shaped cutting edge directly in line with the nail on your forefinger. The point should then effectively remove a thin sliver of plastic as it cuts. (See the photos – it is a lot easier to show you than to describe). As you can see. I have a scraperboard nib taped to the wrong end of a pencil. Not only does this save the expense of a purpose made holder(!), but also allows you to mark out and scribe without changing tools. If you haven't used this handy little tool before, get some scraps of plastic card and practice away. Try varying the pressure and the angle of the nib, you will soon see how different types of stone can be copied. Also try using a steel rule to create coursed stone and try scribing freehand as if you are representing rubble walling. Finally, by experimenting with the scraperboard tool, you can engrave a surface finish and add texture to the stonework. Hopefully by now you will by ready to have a go for real.

With the main features completed, other areas of stonework can be

scribed in until the whole elevation is covered. You can, if you wish, mark the individual stones or courses before you scribe them in, I used to do this when I first started but, after a few models, found that you soon get the hang of how, in this instance, coursed rubble stonework is put together. Whatever happens don't be put off by thinking this process is far too tedious to even bother about. I find that small areas of scribing can often be fitted in between other modelling jobs, making the whole process much less of a chore and ultimately quite rewarding at the end of the day. To finish off, I lightly scrape and score the flat surface of the plastic until you end up with a realistic textured and weathered finish to the walls.

It is interesting to note that many types of stone walling can even be found in different locations of the same building. At least three styles exist on various parts of my Royal Oak prototype ranging from the rubble walls of the main building to evenly coursed stone blocks in the right wing and the larger rounded stones of the rear elevation.

Once scribing is complete, take a sharp craft knife and carefully remove the centre area of each window and door aperture leaving about 3mm to

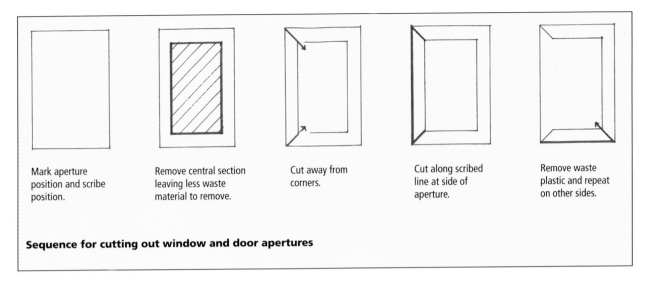

| Mark aperture position and scribe position. | Remove central section leaving less waste material to remove. | Cut away from corners. | Cut along scribed line at side of aperture. | Remove waste plastic and repeat on other sides. |

**Sequence for cutting out window and door apertures**

trim on the inner/waste side of the marked opening. This is not strictly speaking essential, but it does make the plastic easier to cut. Now take the knife and cut a line that bisects the point of each corner. Next, using the steel rule as a guide, remove one side of each aperture at a time remembering always cut away from rather than into each corner wherever possible. This really is where a new knife blade will reap dividends by leaving a clean, crisply-cut edge. With the first opening complete, move on to repeat the process time-and-time-again until all of the apertures have been successfully cut out.

Unlike most ordinary buildings, my stone-built station building's windows have curved, arched tops. In an attempt to get the shape of the arches just right I decided to make a simple jig using the end of a strip of 40 thou thick brass sheet. Having roughly transferred the arc shape from the drawing and photographs to the brass using a pair of dividers, I trimmed and filed away the surplus material until I was completely happy with the resulting shape. With some eighteen arches to make, this simple tool certainly came in handy, particularly as it could be used as a curved ruler for marking out the wall apertures and as a template for cutting around while making window components.

While the walls are still flat, it is always a lot easier to cut out the walls to their final size and add some of the fine detailing, such as windows, projecting cills, lintels and the like from plastic strip. With the exception of advising the novice scratch-builder to take his time, the only other tip is to ensure, as always, that you make sure that your knife is sharp and that a steel straight edge is used wherever possible.

## Stone Features And Window Surrounds

With such a diversity of building design found in this country, it is no surprise that there are countless varieties of stone features, surrounds and architectural embellishments that are often found detailing walls and windows on both stone and brick-based buildings. Examples range from the plain and simple (which can be easily scribed) to the intricately carved and moulded types that often adorn medieval churches and the more ornate buildings.

As is always the case, the first type of stone window surrounds I made for the Bluebell Inn on my layout just

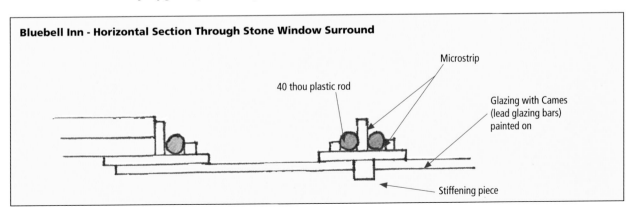

**Bluebell Inn - Horizontal Section Through Stone Window Surround**

Microstrip

40 thou plastic rod

Glazing with Cames (lead glazing bars) painted on

Stiffening piece

happened to be a bit more complicated and difficult to make than those on the station that I constructed some 16 or so years later. Perhaps I should have heeded my own advice and stuck to an easier prototype at the time! At a first glance the intricate nature of the carved stone blocks looks very hard to copy in 4mm scale, however, if carried out in a number of relatively easy stages, the so-called problem can soon be solved. I found, admittedly more by experimentation than design, that the following basic method was reasonably successful and could be applied to many contrasting types of stone feature. If we take a look at both examples you will soon see, in general terms, how a few simple materials can be used to replicate all sorts of features from ornate stone plinths and cornices to window cills, jambs and the like.

In the accompanying diagrams, you can see the basic parts that go together to make up the stone mullions, jambstones, heads and cills of the Bluebell's window and, more importantly, just how they fit in relation to one another. Having already marked and scribed the flush parts of the surrounding stones as part of the main wall process, and removed the over-sized aperture, the first task is to fix a strip of 10thou plastic card behind the wall. Similar material is then used to make the

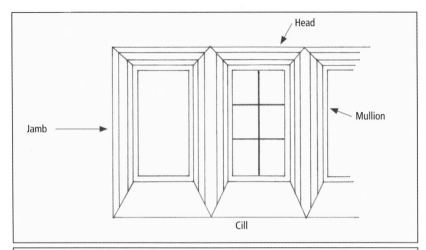

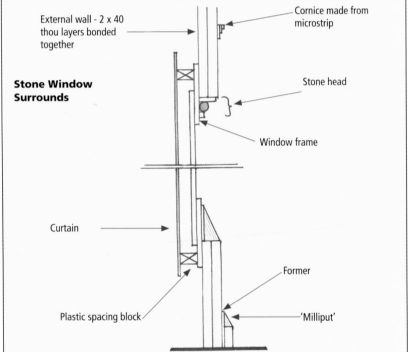

**Stone Window Surrounds**

**1 & 2.** The Bluebell's stone window surrounds in both prototype and model form.

backing to the vertical divisions known as mullions. Next add a combination of various square and rectangular lengths of micro strip and micro rod to represent the moulded stone blocks that make up the surround in real life, taking great care in cutting and fitting them to finish with neat mitres at all intersections.

Now comes the awkward bit! The sloping or more correctly termed weathered cills initially presented me with slightly more of a problem than the rest. At first I attempted these by carefully filing them from plastic, but with results far from consistent, I looked elsewhere for a new method. Eventually, inspired by the fillet of putty I was replacing on the kitchen window, I came up with the idea of using Milliput modelling putty splayed across various layers of plastic card. By adding an additional strip of thin plastic across the inside edge to the back of the cill detail, I effectively made a trowelling margin. To give the putty a better chance of adhering, it is a good idea to key the surface of the plastic card by drilling a few small holes using a pin vice. The Milliput can then be spread firmly over the surface using an old modelling knife blade, making sure that it is pressed firmly into the holes as you do so. To give the surface a nice smooth finish, I found by trial and error, that a spot of water on the blade as it makes the final pass over the putty, is all that was needed to achieve good consistent results. Having set the parts aside so that the Milliput can thoroughly harden overnight, any tiny bits of surplus putty remaining can soon be scraped away to complete the job.

In contrast, even though the stone station's windows were a lot less ornate, they were still fairly awkward to replicate as they comprised both weathered jambs and heads as well as cills and featured an arched shape similar to those often spotted on a church.

As already mentioned I decided to

**1.** Having scribed the stone walls the window aperture is ready for detailing.

**2.** To give the effected of carved stone surrounds, strips of plastic are attached to the rear of the facing sheet to give an aperture the true size of the window and a sill from plastic strip is also added.

**3.** The rebate formed around each window is filled with 'Milliput' modelling putty which is smoothed off to give a neat appearance.

**4.** Stone courses are cut into the dry 'Milliput' as the casement window takes shape.

make a special brass tool in an attempt to get the shape of the arches just right and more importantly consistent with one another. With some eighteen arches to make, this simple gadget certainly came in handy, particularly as it could be used as a curved ruler for marking out the wall apertures and again here as

a template for cutting around while making window components. Just as I did with the earlier window cills made for the Bluebell Inn, the station's splayed or weathered stone window surround sections were formed by spreading 'Milliput' into a rebate formed in the plastic card walls before the windows

**1.** This ornate Dutch gable with coping and a finial can be found on the LNWR station at Wansford on the Nene Valley Railway.

**2.** This simple but effective window overlooks the ECML at Little Bytham.

3. Hunstanton's Town Hall features some interesting embellishments.

4. This type of decoration is often found on banks and high street shops.

**5.** This unusual tower crowns Stamford's Midland station.

**6.** Here's something different to model! The Triangular Lodge at Rushton overlooks the Midland main line.

(which are detailed in a separate section of this book) were added behind.

Having now described a couple of different window surround types, I am sure you will be able to grasp the general principles involved on making these and pretty much any other stonework details and embellishments. If you find something slightly different don't be put off, experiment and have a trial run or two, as I did initially. I still think that one of the most enjoyable aspects of this hobby is to try out new ways of making things, so remember these notes are not prescriptive, part of the fun is adapting the basic concept to suit your own circumstances. If you make something that is not particularly successful put it to one side for a day or two and try again. I am sure you will find it highly rewarding when eventually your trials work out well. Opposite are a few interesting prototype details to inspire you to have a go!

## Backing/Strengthening

To strengthen the model, and to prevent it from warping, it is a good idea to back the walls with a second sheet of 40 thou plastic card. This layer is marked out in much the same way as the first but, as you can see from the photos, allowances need to be made to ensure you end up with a neat butt-joint at the corners. Now I

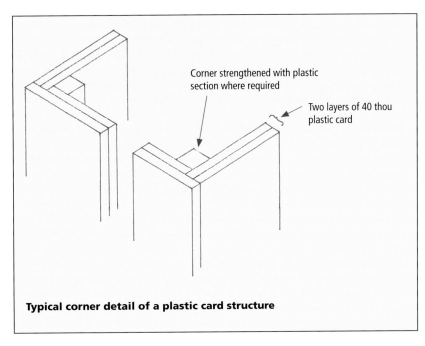

Corner strengthened with plastic section where required

Two layers of 40 thou plastic card

**Typical corner detail of a plastic card structure**

am aware that many modellers have had problems with plastic card warping or twisting in the past but fortunately, touch wood, the use of two-ply laminated plastic card walls and a rigid internal framework seems to have eliminated it from my models, the oldest of which is now approaching 28 years old. I was once told that the key to avoid any warping is to ensure that both layers are of identical thickness so as to equalise any possible movement. If you look at the photo on page 18 that I took of an early experiment with a 15 thou and 30 thou

laminations you can clearly see the less than satisfactory result!

Before fixing the backing layer in place behind the outer wall, carefully mark out and remove over-sized window apertures that will clear the plastic window surrounds and window frame strips that will be fitted to the back of the scribed wall sections. Next drill a number of holes throughout the backing layer to allow 'Mek Pak' solvent to be brushed into the laminated joint. This will result in a much better bond than that achieved by merely running it around the edges alone.

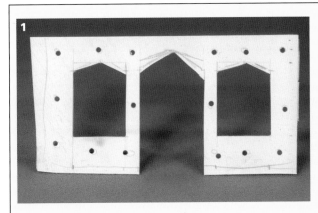

**1.** The backing layer is cut out and holes are drilled in it to allow solvent to penetrate between the sheets.

**2.** The backing layer is positioned behind the main wall once all of the windows and surrounds are in place.

The Bluebell Inn is seen on the author's Paston Ridings layout.

Above and far right: Three shots of the Bluebell Inn during construction.

Having decided to make a model of this fascinating stone-built pub, I firstly visited my local museum and reference library to research and authenticate my model to the 1930s era. Although the main building hasn't changed much since the '20s, I unearthed numerous old photos and maps that not only helped to date the pub's various extensions, but also showed even more thatched cottages, since demolished, on either side of the main building. More by luck than by judgement, I came across a local historian who was kind enough to lend me his collection of photos, which, amongst other things, included one of the outbuildings behind the pub, demolished in 1961.

My findings revealed that the present pub was extended around 1923 and is reputed to be the oldest pub in Peterborough, with parts dating from the 16th century; its imposing stone front once dominating the old farming village of Dogsthorpe which, incidentally, is now totally engulfed by the ever expanding city. As you can see, several new wings have been tacked on over the years, so together with the assortment of outbuildings,

The prototype pub in Dogsthorpe, Peterborough.

the Bluebell, along with its neighbouring cottages, gave the challenge of modelling a scene that featured almost all forms of building construction.

Why Bluebell and not Blue Bell as the pub sign shows? Well it always had bluebells on the sign when I was a lad!

# RENDERED WALLS

A GWR Prairie tank shunts tank wagons in front of Moreton in Marsh's render clad creamery.

Many buildings have walls covered in various kinds of smooth or textured cement and sand render. Sometimes known as pebbledash, this is an easy medium to copy on almost any kind of model building.

One of the earliest forms of render was wattle and daub, that was commonly used to fill in the walls between the structural timber framework of early buildings. Since those days render has drifted both in and out of fashion as the centuries come and go. Historically render was widely used to give old buildings a facelift, much earlier timber framed structures were, for example, often rendered to give them a more 'modern' appearance in Georgian

**1.** A typical rendered end terrace gable.

England. Indeed in some places render was, and still is, applied, scored and tooled to give the appearance of a much more expensive stone building. Regional variations, such as the highly decorative pargetting form of rendering seen in parts of Essex, make this medium a very interesting and colourful way of weatherproofing cottages and shops. In more modern times rendering is often used to provide a weatherproof surface finish to unfaced masonry walls, such as those made from common bricks and, more recently, concrete blocks. It is also widely used by architects to provide contrasting coloured panels to enhance their designs.

From the modeller's perspective there are a number of pretty straightforward ways to make rendered walls, they are:
• Applying a gritty material to the walls
• Treating the plastic surface to give a fine rendered appearance
• Scribing walls where a 'mock stone' effect is required

When I was at school and had a Saturday job in my local model shop I remember reading Allan Downes' method of using budgie grit to cover a card building to represent a coarse type of pebble-dashed render. I knew therefore that it wasn't going to be too difficult to do, but the problem was, I soon discovered, how to get sand to stick successfully to my preferred plastic card medium. After a bit of trial and error, using various types of solvents and adhesives, I eventually came up with a very simple method of representing a medium texture render using fine foundry sand and liquid polystyrene solvent.

Having made the external wall from the customary two plain sheets of 40 thou plastic card and fitted all the windows, doors, sills and added any decorations, the basic method is to take a No.3 size paintbrush loaded with Daywat Poly and carefully spread a generous amount of solvent on the wall. Then, quickly, before the solvent has chance to evaporate, sprinkle on a thin layer of

**2.** Render is often applied in conjunction with brick and other finishes.

**3.** Traditionally render was used as an infill between an exposed timber frame.

**4.** Render is often used to give the impression that the building is faced in stone.

**1.** Fine sand is scattered and pressed into the softened plastic sheet.

**2.** Once the solvent has dried, any surplus grit can be brushed off.

foundry sand and immediately press it down onto the surface. Hopefully the sand will embed itself in the tacky surface and will, within seconds, have stuck firmly in place. When you are happy that the solvent has dried, tap the model to release any loose sand and all, as they say, will be revealed. Being pretty volatile, the solvent rapidly evaporates from the plastic card once it has been applied. This means that, in most instances, a large wall cannot be coated in one continuous area. I found from experience that it is far better to cover a small area of wall at a time and repeat the process over and over again, carefully avoiding all details that in real life are un-rendered, until the whole wall has been evenly covered. Finally after the surface has been left to harden overnight, remove any excess sand that has not

been fully bonded to the surface of the wall and paint and weather with matt enamels to represent the prototype.

For rougher textured renders, you can simply use a coarser sand or grit. As a word of warning, I would suggest that you try out any type of sand or grit on a piece of scrap plastic before attempting to cover a model. Not only does this check that the solvent can successfully hold the material in place but also prevents the disaster of a potentially ruined model if the method goes wrong.

When I started modelling the creamery at Morton-in-Marsh, I was intending to represent the cement and sand render by applying sand directly to the plastic walls, just has I had done on the Methodist chapel on my layout some years ago. As a check to see what it would look like I

spread some liquid solvent over a scrap of plastic card and, while it was still wet, scattered on some fine sand. Having pressed it down, let it dry and brushed away the excess sand, I could see that the method was still a pretty good one, but the finish was perhaps if anything a little too gritty to represent the fine rendered finish of the creamery.

Another idea I had, again some time ago, but hadn't yet given it a go, was to once again wet the surface of the plastic with solvent and firmly press fine wet and dry paper into it, let it dry for a while before peeling off the paper and leaving the newly created surface texture to harden. To my surprise, my first attempts didn't look too bad at all and, after a bit more experimentation with various grades of abrasive paper, I was pretty

**3.** Abrasive paper is stuck down and pressed into the plastic card surface.

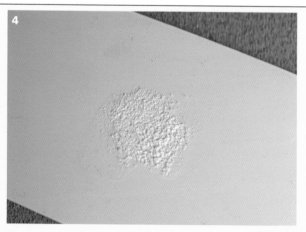

**4.** When peeled off, the surface resembles cement and sand render.

This coarse textured pre-cast concrete building can be made using a combination of scribing and render techniques. **Photo: Keith Parkinson**

happy with the results and it wasn't long before I was applying the finish to the model's otherwise plain plastic walls. When set solid, the surface was found to be generally good but I did notice a few rough areas and blemishes that had to be rubbed over with the same wet and dry paper that created it before I was totally satisfied with the finish.

To the model-maker the render used to look like 'mock stone' simply features the same types of courses as found on real stone buildings. Being predominantly regular in pattern, the applied courses are very quick and easy to represent in model form by simply scribing them onto the surface of plastic sheet in exactly the same way as we have seen for stonework earlier in this book. If the surface is textured why not try the wet and dry paper method mentioned above as well?

## Concrete Structures

When it comes to concrete walls it is fair to say that the surface will either be smooth, lightly textured or, in the case of an exposed aggregate finish, just as gritty as an applied render. Luckily for the model maker, this means that the

same techniques used for render can be applied when scratch-building structures of this type.

Quite often railway companies have widely employed pre-fabricated pre-cast concrete structures as accommodation for permanent way gangs, gatekeepers, signalling and telegraph staff and the like. If you take a look at the prototype

photos you will see that buildings of this type are, in fact, almost identical from a modelling perspective as timber buildings but they have a gritty textured surface. The answer is again simple, scribe the lines to represent the precast concrete planks, add plastic strip for the framing and treat the surface just as you would for rendered walls. Easy isn't it?

This smaller pre-cast concrete platelayers' hut has a smoother surface finish. **Photo: Keith Parkinson**

A Great Western railcar awaits departure from Shipston-on-Stour.

Historically, timber has been at the centre of almost all major forms of building construction, being used in both framed and clad structures from the earliest of times. As timber is a quick and economical way of constructing all sorts of structures such as stations, signal boxes and huts, many standard, often pre-fabricated, buildings of this type can be found along the lineside. It is therefore, in my opinion, well worth giving them some consideration in the pages of this book.

Although you might well find medieval timber framed houses and barns beside the railway in some parts of the country, most wooden buildings used by the main railway companies from the industrial revolution onwards tend to comprise a regular framework

of larger section timbers in association with thinner boarding or planking that acts as a weatherproof cladding either around or between the main components of the framework.

Some forms of timber frame, like those found in old barns and sheds, are totally concealed and as such do not even need to be considered by the modelmaker. Others, such as those widely used in the construction of wooden stations and signal boxes, are exposed and have panels of decorative cladding that fill the gaps between the structural members.

If you look carefully, you will find that there are several types of cladding found on lineside structures, the more common ones are:

• Tongued, grooved and vee jointed

boarding, which comprises interlocking planks of wood that give the wall a flush face. These are very easily portrayed in model form by simply scribing parallel lines on a sheet of plain plastic card.

• Shiplap boarding is similar, but as the name suggests has the appearance of a clinker built boat with planks always overlapping those on the row below. I usually model this type of wall using either microstrip or 3mm wide strips, cut from 10thou plastic card, stuck in overlapping rows onto a base of 40 thou plastic card.

• Waney edged boarding is much the same as shiplap but is much more rustic, featuring planks with exposed bark edges. These are cut freehand, again from 10 thou plastic sheet, but with one edge trimmed to an angle to represent

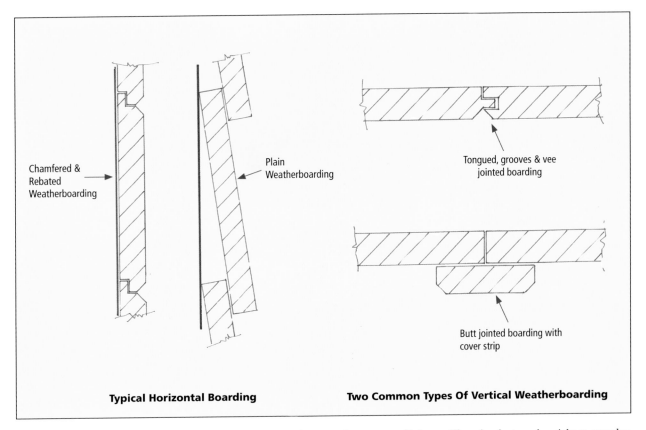

Chamfered & Rebated Weatherboarding

Plain Weatherboarding

Tongued, grooves & vee jointed boarding

Butt jointed boarding with cover strip

**Typical Horizontal Boarding**

**Two Common Types Of Vertical Weatherboarding**

the uneven surface of the original.

• Timber shingles are not particularly common in this country. They are in fact wooden tiles, commonly made of stained cedar, which are nailed to timber battens fixed to the outer walls of the building. Often shield-shaped, sheets of similar tiles are available in the Wills range of building components.

• Less common but still worth modelling are log cabins. One particularly attractive example, a clubhouse on the A149 between Kings Lynn and Hunstanton in

Norfolk, has often caught my eye. If I ever attempted a model of such a prototype, I may just be tempted to put the plastic card to one side for a while and make it based around a plywood shell so that wood glue could be used throughout. Just like the real thing it could be covered with logs – well perhaps not, specially selected straight, dried, twigs would be more appropriate.

When it comes down to making timber structures it is perhaps best to look at few simple-to-make examples.

The simplest and quickest wooden buildings to make are those with large areas of flush timber cladding that is fixed to an internal concealed wooden frame. To do this firstly set out the wall section in pencil as normal and then add a series of equidistant parallel lines where the planks abut. Next check with your prototype photos to ensure that any prominent features are correctly aligned (quite often planks will line up with the heads and cills of windows. If no further adjustment to the setting out

**1.** Horizontal boarding.

**2.** Vertical boarding.

**3.** This rustic boarding is widely found on all types of rural buildings.

is needed, take a steel rule and a scraperboard tool and firmly scribe along the pencil lines locating the joints in the boarding. Now turn the wall upside down and scribe the line again from the other side. This will clean out any plastic flash from the groove and give the scribed line a neat even appearance.

To make the outer layer of the timber walls for Shipston Station, start the process by marking out the basic outline of the front and the two end walls side-by-side on a sheet of 40 thou plastic card. Then add all of the main horizontal and vertical lines that will locate the thicker timber members and represent the building's timber frame. Using appropriately sized plastic strip (from the Evergreen range), start to add the framing to the first wall by cutting individual parts to length and sticking them in position with solvent. The eagle-eyed amongst you will notice from the photos that I chose to leave off the outermost members of the framing until after the model was partly assembled. This is a simple method of ensuring that the correct spacing of vertical members is maintained between panels at the corners, where it is not as easy to work out the exact centres until the corner framework is in place. With the main thicker sections in place, the jointing strips within the panels can be added from much finer section microstrip.

Now, you may think that we have gone tearing away without cutting out the window and door openings. Ok, I will readily admit that I usually prefer to cut these out before adding any detail at all, but in this case, largely as many of the timber members that frame the doors and walls are only a couple of millimetres wide, I feel that a slightly different approach makes things a lot easier in the long run.

Having stuck down the polystyrene strip representing the framework and set the assembly aside to harden overnight, the window apertures are best removed in two stages. Firstly make a cut about

**1.** This typical horizontal boarded LNWR shelter is at the Nene Valley Railway.

**2.** Timber framing and vertical boarding GWR style.

**3.** This Midland signal box has both horizontal and vertical boarding.

**4.** Vertical planking at Minffordd on the Ffestiniog Railway.

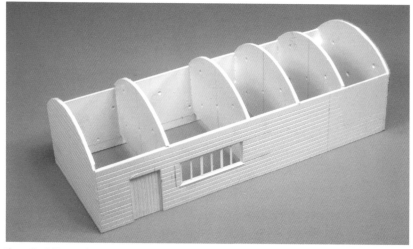

The walls of this wooden structure have simply been scribed onto the outer layer of the plastic card walls.

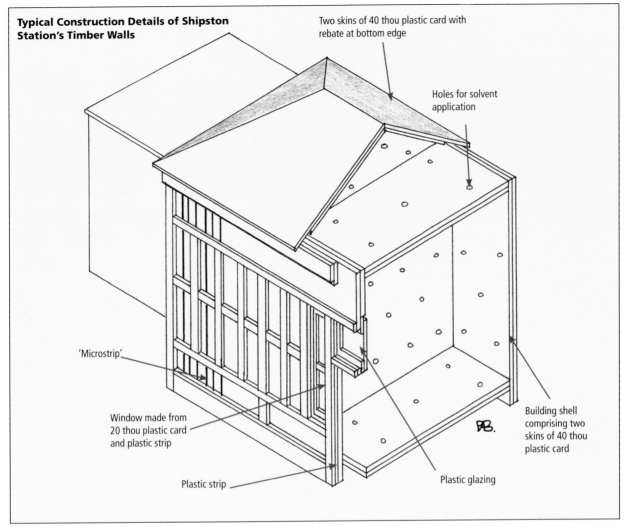

**Typical Construction Details of Shipston Station's Timber Walls**

Two skins of 40 thou plastic card with rebate at bottom edge

Holes for solvent application

'Microstrip'

Window made from 20 thou plastic card and plastic strip

Plastic strip

Plastic glazing

Building shell comprising two skins of 40 thou plastic card

This lean-to extension features rustic waney-edge boarding.

1.5-2mm around the inside edge of the opening, which is then removed. By using the positioned framing as a guide for the knife, next carefully trim away the remaining plastic. You will have to be very careful to make sure that you don't cut into the plastic strip, but you do end up with both window and door openings that are exactly the right size. Simple isn't it? I suppose you could, if you prefer, laboriously mark out the holes on the backing sheet and cut them out prior to fixing the plastic framing, but I bet that this would take a lot longer to get right, especially as, on this prototype, some of the bits left between adjacent openings are so very narrow. Before moving on to the next stage, quickly rub around the edges with a small file, which

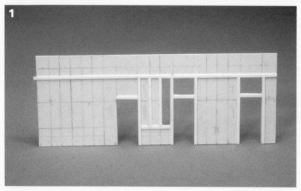

**1.** The first lengths of plastic strip have been added to the marked out sheet of 40 thou plastic. Some, but not all, of the windows have been cut out.

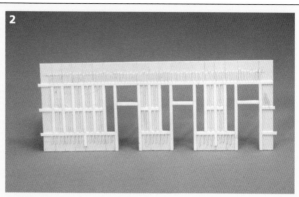

**2.** The bulk of the larger section plastic strip has been added, the windows have all been cut out and most of the smaller section micro strip is in place. Note that the ends have not been trimmed yet.

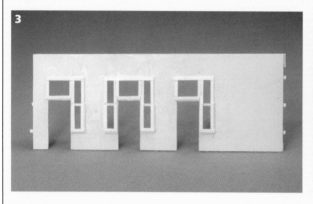

**3.** The various lengths of plastic strip that make up the timber windows are added to the back of the wall.

**4.** With the windows now in position, the horizontal timber members to the top and bottom of the wall are added.

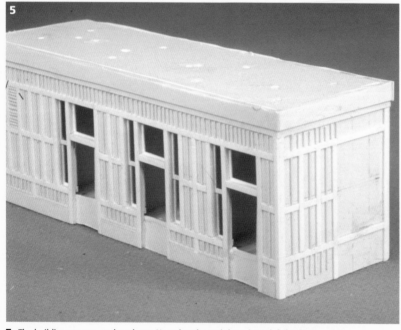

**5.** The building structure takes shape. Note that the ends have been left for the time being.

ensures that all cut surfaces are left with a clean and tidy edge.

In our second example, a Midland Railway station building (based on a Gloucestershire prototype), the construction process is very similar except that the planks need to be marked and scribed just as we did with the shed, before the projecting plastic strips are added to represent the timber framework.

It is worth remembering, from a construction technology point of view, that the upright timber frame members usually run full height with the horizontal timbers running between them. There can of course be exceptions to the rule so, as always, don't forget to take a close look at your prototype photos and drawings before you begin.

RIGHT: This sketch shows how the Midland station building at Haresfield in Gloucestershire can be represented by partly scribing the walls with plastic card strips added to form the framework.

BELOW: Haresfield station building.

BOTTOM: This mock timber framed cottage is simply represented by sticking plastic strip onto a solid plastic card structure.

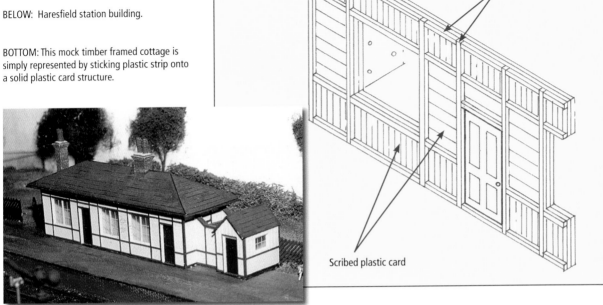

Backing layer of 40 thou plastic card

Plastic section

Scribed plastic card

A small Great Western Prairie and 'B Set' arrive at the completed Shipston-on-Stour station on the late Michael Warner's impressive 00 gauge layout.

The third member of the Shipston trio is a small timber framed station building comprising a modest waiting room, ticket office, the usual toilets, and a simple, but attractive canopy. With only limited photographic information and just a few dimensions taken from old site plans, I prepared a drawing as near as possible to 4mm scale. Although you might think this

would be reasonably straightforward, it wasn't as easy as I had first hoped. The terminus end was widely photographed in its heyday so getting the details I needed was relatively easy. Unfortunately pictures of the opposite end, I found to my dismay, were at a premium. I knew there was a small toilet block on this end but details were very sketchy indeed. Luckily a side-on

photo of this end of the building eventually turned up and gave me pretty much all of the remaining details that were needed to fill in the gaps in my drawing.

## Walls

With planning complete, I started construction of the station by marking out the basic outline of the front and the

**1.** The first stage of assembly sees the first two wall sections being joined together.

**2.** The dividing walls and floor sections are added.

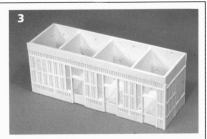

**3.** The framework around the corners has been started.

**4.** The Gent's toilet wing is added to the station building.

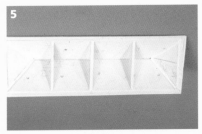

**5.** This view of the underside of the roof structure shows how it fits together.

**6.** The addition of the roof makes it look more like the completed structure.

two end walls side by side on a sheet of 40 thou plastic card. I then added all of the main horizontal and vertical lines that locate the thicker timber members that will represent the building's timber frame. Using appropriately sized plastic strip (from the Evergreen range), I started to add the framing to the first wall, cutting individual parts to length and sticking them in position with 'Mek-Pak' solvent. The eagle-eyed amongst you will notice from the photos that I left off the outermost members until after the model was partly assembled. This was just a simple way of ensuring that the correct spacing was maintained between panels at the corners where it is not as easy to work out the centres until the corner framework is in place.

As you can see in the section on Timber Building, the timber framing was then added before the appertures for the windows and doors were cut out.

## Windows and doors

Windows, as can be seen from the illustrations, are simply made up in a very similar way from individual lengths of plastic strip stuck in place behind the apertures that had already been cut out from the card. In order to make things as easy as possible, the edges of the openings were painted with the frame colour, which in this case was brown, before the plastic glazing was cut to size and glued to the back of the door or window.

The panelled doors on the other hand, were very simple to make using laminated layers of plastic card. As elsewhere the boarded infill sections were created using a scraper board tool.

## Assembly

As you can see from the illustrations, assembly of the main body of the building was in this instance, very straightforward indeed. With a false floor, internal dividing walls and roof base, a sturdy structure was very quickly made up from the basic building block; namely two layers of 40thou plastic sheet laminated together. The resulting model ends up with considerable strength and rigidity which prevents it from warping.

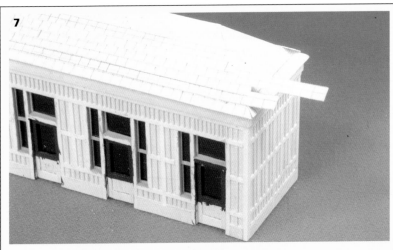

**7.** The first few rows of paper slates are seen in position.

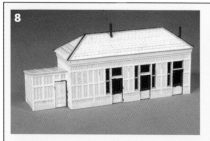

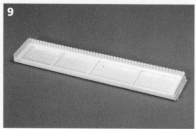

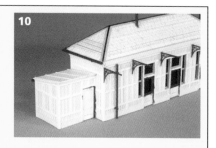

**8.** With the slates covering the roof, the ridge and hip tiles are added from plastic rod and the remnants of an old brown envelope sent to me by the Editor!

**9.** Seen from below, the canopy is once again of plastic construction with a Slater's awning.

**10.** In this close-up the D&S awning brackets and scratch-built brass rainwater goods can be clearly seen.

**11.** The completed building prior to painting.

## Roof

Once again construction of the roof employed the same basic skills and methods that I have already described in detail. The hipped ends are, as you might expect, a little trickier and time consuming than a roof with simple verges however they shouldn't really create any problems to a newcomer to scratch-building.

Strips of artist's watercolour paper were used for the slates, largely for its much better textured appearance and for the ease that it can be trimmed to the hipped angles, whereas strips of plastic rod were used to create the raised section of the ridge and hip tiles with thin strips of thick paper either side to represent the flat bits.

## Canopy

Having found that Stater's make some nice, clean injection-moulded GWR awning fascias of exactly the right pattern for Shipston, the canopy structure was really a piece of cake to put together, I used my customary laminated plastic card core method with plastic strip of various sizes and sections to finish it off. With the basic element complete the canopy was solvent-welded in place with the aid of a few brass pegs that I had introduced along the joint line to give it extra support.

In reality, five decorative cast iron brackets actually supported the canopy. Despite looking virtually everywhere that I could think of in my search for suitable scale representations, I initially drew a blank. Still thinking of other possible sources I decided to trawl through a heap of old catalogues and price lists that were lurking in a drawer in my workshop. In the pile was an old D&S list. To my delight I found that they supply an etched-brass bracket of pretty much the same size and shape and indeed almost identical to the ones that I needed. Ok, so they weren't of Great Western origin and the pattern of the infill wasn't exactly right, but tucked right up underneath the canopy and awning it would be very difficult to notice the difference. Without further ado I sent my order off and pressed on with the rainwater goods while I was waiting for them to arrive.

When they came, I decided to make a slight modification and soldered two small pegs made from brass wire onto the top and bottom of the vertical part of each bracket. Making sure that the pegs were not on the exposed side of the end brackets, I marked their positions one by one on the plastic walls and then drilled through using a small clearance drill in a pin vice. Once the brackets had been primed with a coat of car primer, a few well-placed spots of epoxy resin soon secured them into their final positions and the canopy was complete.

## Rainwater goods and Chimneys

With almost everything else made from plastic of one kind or another, I was very tempted to make the rainwater gutters and pipes for this model from 'Plastruct' or similar plastic components as well. As I have experienced damage to plastic representations of these items in the past, I decided, however, to make them from brass. Similarly, brass tubing was used to make the thin chimneys that protrude through the slate roof. As with the canopy brackets, all of the metal parts were thoroughly cleaned up with a fibre brush, primed and fixed into position in locating holes carefully drilled in the plastic building structure.

## Painting

As already mentioned, I usually apply a couple of coats of red oxide aerosol car primer to the metal parts just before they are fixed into position. This will of course help the paint to stick to them and will also save a lot of masking off, necessary if they were to be sprayed in-situ.

As you can see from the photos, most of the building was painted using only two colours. The walls, being predominantly cream, were given a couple of coats of Precision/Phoenix 'GWR Stone No.l' (P21) whereas the doors, contrasting framework and rainwater goods were finished in Revell 'Matt Brown' (M84). The only exception were the roofing slates. These, as you might have already guessed, were painted in various shades of matt grey from the Humbrol and Perkins ranges.

## Conclusion

Although one or two elements of construction could be deemed a bit tricky to the uninitiated, I am sure you will agree that there is really nothing that is too difficult about scratch-building a reasonably straightforward model such as this. Hopefully by now you will be having a few ideas for a project of your own, if not please read on.

This image depicts a disused Shipston-on-Stour station prior to its demolition. Michael Warner Collection

A rural scene on Paston Ridings.

Basically, from the construction technology point of view, timber windows fall into two main categories, namely casement windows and sash windows.

Casement windows usually comprise a main framework that is sized to fit the opening formed in the wall. Onto this frame, one or more glazed sub-frames are hinged to make up the opening lights, whilst the non-opening apertures are simply fitted with glass. These are known as the fixed lights. Opening lights can vary, depending upon the way they are hinged to the frame; top hung, side hung, bottom hung and centrally pivoted are some of the most common forms found. In reality the timber sections that are used to make up this type of windows are rebated both for the frames to fit into each other (preventing water ingress) and also to hold the panes of glass, usually in conjunction with wooden beads or putty. For the modeller, this means that the opening lights will sit slightly proud of the main window frame on a typical window.

Sash windows were very popular in Victorian times so it is not surprising that they were widely favoured by many railway companies who were building their stations and offices at that time. The main difference between these and casement windows is that the opening lights slide up and down vertically within channels in the frame instead of opening outwards. When modelling sash windows, the one thing you really need to remember is that the upper sliding sash needs to be fitted on the outside of the lower one.

**1.** A typical casement cottage window.

**2.** This is from a GWR yard office.

**3.** A top hung window.

**4.** This version is finer and much more ornate.

**5.** Typical metal French windows.

**6.** A simple sash window.

**7.** This LNWR sash is much more complicated than the norm.

**8.** Some windows are fitted with security bars.

**9.** This sash window has an unusual head detail.

**10.** Modern windows still follow the same principles.

## Casement Windows

To make a casement window from scratch, start by cutting some 4mm wide strips of 10 thou plastic card ensuring that the edges are perfectly straight. Take one of these strips, cut it to length (about 8mm longer than the opening), and glue it to the inside face of the top of the first window opening so that it projects approximately 1mm inwards from the edge of the opening when viewed from the front. In the case of the arched window on my stone station, this was made from two sections cut to the same curvature as the arch using the same homemade jig used to cut out the apertures. Next, cut two more strips of the same material to fit the sides of the aperture and similarly fix them in place.

Plastic strip can be used to make a simple casement window.

Having let the solvent harden for a while, it is now time to prepare the bottom end of the two uprights, ready for the addition of the fourth frame member. Carefully mark the position of the top edge of the frame member (ie: 1mm above the bottom of the aperture) and make a couple of cuts to mark the waste area of the two side strips. Once you are perfectly happy that these are in the right place, the strip below can then be removed completely. Now offer up a strip of 10 thou plastic card and check that the bottom frame member is both square and level. If not, take a fine sliver or two from one of the sides, as fine adjustment before finally sticking the part in place. Ok, I know this does sound a bit long winded, but it is in practice very quick to do, and is certainly a lot easier than cutting out all of those individual frames.

Moving on, the next task is to add the vertical frame divisions (mullions) and the horizontal frame divisions (transoms) from thinner strips of 10 thou plastic card. This effectively completes the basic window frame ready for the addition of the opening lights. In the closed position these are best represented by gluing lengths of 10 thou plastic strip to the outer face of the main frame. Once again start with the top member of each, then the sides, and finally trim the sides to ensure the bottom section is in the correct position. When complete, paint the exposed edges of the window frames

**1.** The first stage in making a casement window is to line the top and three sides.

**2.** The bottom section is added next.

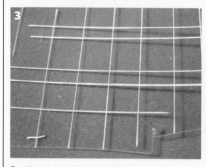

**3.** Glazing beads can be drawn in paint on clear plastic glazing material.

**4.** The glazing is cut out and glued behind the window.

with matt enamel paints and set aside to dry while you prepare the glazing.

To glaze the windows, cut small pieces of clear plastic to size and very carefully fix them in place, taking great care not to use too much solvent. You will soon learn how far the liquid cement will travel by capillary action through this material, so it should be reasonably easy to avoid any squeezing out onto the surface of the

window proper. Where the window's lights are divided up into individual panes by glazing, you can either represent these by using tiny pieces of microstrip cut to suit every location or, as I prefer, paint them on the back of the clear glazing using a bow pen, a straight edge and some enamel paint to match the rest of the window frame.

## Sash Windows

Sash windows are, funnily enough, made using pretty much the same general techniques but in a slightly different way. In this case, you start with the four sides of the outer frame exactly as you would the casement variety, but then add the top and two sides of the upper sliding frame section. This is trimmed in the same way as already described, to take a length of plastic strip representing the bottom of the frame. Next plastic strips of the same thickness as the frame are fixed in place below the top frame and along the bottom. These are set back from the front edge of the outer frame

**1-3 .** These three shots of the ex-LNWR building from Barnwell, now at Wansford on the NVR, show the close up detail of a sash window.

and will give the appearance of the groove in which the upper window sash slides. Finally, the bottom sliding sash is made up and fitted in exactly the same way, before the clear glazing and glazing bars are added to complete the window.

To add a bit more realism to your building, try modelling a few windows in the open position. Whether sash windows or casements, it is fairly easy to adapt the method of construction to create a realistic looking scene.

During my research, I have often found that window types can vary considerably on differing parts of the same building. This is worth looking out for, particularly when you have a fair idea that your prototype has been modified, refurbished or extended over the years. Here, as elsewhere, I just can't stress enough the importance of a good set of reference photographs. Don't be afraid to carefully study each window in turn and, if you think it is going to help, make sketches of any differences that you find.

## Dormer Windows

When a building has a room inside the roof space light is usually drawn in through either a roof window such as the modern 'Velux' variety often used in loft conversions, or more commonly in a dormer window.

Roof windows are relatively easy to model, being merely, as the name suggests, a window in the roof. The only thing that we as modellers do need to bear in mind is exactly how the window unit sits in relation to the roof slope and also how its surrounding metal flashings that prevent rainwater from penetrating the building are detailed. Take a close look at the real thing, you will soon see what I mean.

Dormer windows on the other hand need a little more work to replicate in model form. The best way to model dormers, I find, is to pre-assemble a complete window and fit it to the dormer cheeks that protrude through the roof slope. I usually start by making the front part of the window frame from

**1.** The first stages of a sliding sash window from the rear showing the strips of plastic being trimmed to size.

**2.** The upper sash is completed by the addition of a length of plastic strip.

**3.** The completed upper sash from the back showing the strips of plastic that represent the groove in which it would slide.

**4.** The lower sash is added ready for glazing bars and decoration.

**5.** The lower sash from behind.

**6.** The completed painted and glazed window assembly.

20 thou sheet cut to size with an aperture removed for the window. To this I add the rest of the window parts in more or less the same way as already detailed. The completed window can now be fixed in place between dormer cheeks (again made from 20 thou plastic card) which are positioned and secured

at right angles to the dummy first floor. Having added the curtains and painted the inside of the roof space a dark colour, to avoid seeing any unsightly bits of white plastic on the completed model, a sub-roof can finally be fitted above the dormer in readiness for the main roofing process to begin.

**1.** Dormer windows are a common feature of thatched cottages.

**2.** The model version is essentially a window with plastic 'cheeks'.

## Metal Windows

Whether constructed from cast iron or more recently steel or aluminium, metal windows are widely found in domestic and commercial situations ranging from cottages and houses, through to schools and shop fronts. Due to their ability to easily fill large openings they have, since the industrial revolution, also been the first-choice window type for all kinds of factories, warehouses and workshops. As the metal frame components are much stronger than their timber counterparts, they are prototypically usually made of much thinner section materials. This should be taken in consideration when chosing the best way to model them.

One way of representing metal windows is to use some of the excellent etched-brass frets that are currently available on the market as long as you can find some just the right size for your model. I find them particularly useful when I have to make a large number of identical units for, say a lineside warehouse or an engine shed. Unless they already have an etched border, I prefer to solder fixing tabs to the outer edges of the etchings made from scraps of brass (usually waste bits from the fret). This enables me to position the window in a rebate made in the wall, rather than fit them to the face of the aperture. Having given them a couple of coats of spray car primer and a lick of paint, I usually fix them in place with a sparing amount of contact adhesive such as 'Evo-Stik' before attaching some clear plastic glazing in the same manner.

When I make the much smaller metal windows needed for a cottage, or the leaded lights that often fit into stone window surrounds, I adopt a quick and relatively easy method of scratch-building. Basically, I start by framing the window aperture as normal, with strips of 20 thou plastic card and then add the vertical members or mullions from plastic strip of the same thickness. Finally I take a sheet of clear plastic glazing material

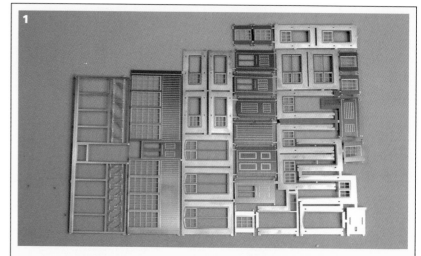

**1.** This window etching from Ambis is for Saxby's Midland Railway station.

**2.** Standard window etchings can, in many instances, be carefully cut and resized.

**3.** This casement window is made from a proprietary injection plastic moulding.

and, using a bowpen, draw lines of undiluted Humbrol paint across it to represent the glazing bars that divide the window up into panes. Once dry, the glazing is carefully stuck to the back of the window with a few spots of solvent.

## Curtains

One thing that many model-makers frequently forget to make and add to their miniature structures are curtains and net curtains.

Ordinary curtains are easily and quickly made up from strips of 10thou plastic strip that have been trimmed and painted to suit. Remember when painting to add a few darker streaks of colour to represent folds in the cloth. If you want your curtains to have a greater three-dimensional effect, a range of vacuum formed drape mouldings, complete with tie backs at the sides, are commercially available from Langley Miniature Models.

To make net curtains, I usually use scraps of material from some old white

**1.** Simple painted curtains can be stuck behind windows using spacers.

**2.** The curtains seen from the viewing side.

stockings or tights that I scrounged from a secretary at work years ago when they were in fashion. As this fabric doesn't look right unless it is stretched, I first make a separate frame of 40 thou plastic card that is slightly larger than the window aperture. I then stretch the stocking material as far as I can over a frame made from Lego building bricks. Having coated the plastic frame with 'Evo-Stik' contact adhesive, it is placed glue side down onto the stretched fabric

and left for a few hours to harden. Once dry to the touch, I usually press the net curtain into the glue, to ensure that it is fully bonded, and trim off the waste material from around the frame.

To give the correct impression of depth, when both type of curtains are fixed behind the windows, I normally use a couple of strips of 2mm thick plastic strip as spacers between the back face of the wall and the top and bottom of the curtaining.

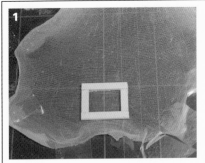

**1.** Net curtains can be made on a separate plastic card frame.

**2.** The frame is them positioned between the window and the normal painted curtains.

**3.** Net curtains in place behind a completed window.

**1.** A GNR timber panelled door.

**2.** This GWR door has a glazed light above it.

**3.** The framing can be more ornate as on the GCR.

**4.** The panelling can be embellished too.

**5.** Glazed panelled doors are widely found.

**6.** Boarded doors can be scribed straight on plastic sheet.

**7.** A classic Georgian front door.

**8.** Two contrasting high street doors.

## Doors

Many types and styles of doors are available to the modelmaker from several of the leading accessory manufacturers. Materials range from cast white metal, injection moulded plastic and etched-brass.

As with commercially produced windows, the only setback with most mass produced doors from the scratch-builder's perspective is that you have to design your model to fit the door sizes available, rather than fit the scale opening to suit your model's prototype dimensions. I will readily admit that glazed doors, having several tiny panes of glass, are probably best represented using these types, as are some of the more ornate patterns that you find on more elegant structures. Plain flush-faced timber framed and panelled or ledged and braced doors of the kind widely found on railway buildings and cottages are on the other hand much easier to model yourself.

To make a basic flush door, take a sheet of 40 thou plastic card and trim one edge to make sure that it is flat. As you can see, I always find good use for my scraps and offcuts of plastic card, this being just one of them. Then, using an engineer's square, simply mark the edges of the door in pencil and add all of the detail, replicating exactly the pattern of the original door. Just as you would with the stone walls, scribe over the pencil lines to leave the framing and panelling. Unless I am modelling an open door, I usually leave about 4mm of plastic around the top and sides of the true door size when I cut it out. This is to enable it to be fixed behind the door frame, which incidentally is made in exactly the same way as for windows. To complete the door, take a short length of plastic strip and file it to represent the weatherboard at the bottom. Trim it to length and carefully solvent-weld it in place.

If one of the panels on your door is glazed, try using clear plastic as the base material instead of plain white. If you want panelling that is deeply moulded, use plastic strip for the framing with squares of plastic cut to shape and filed for the panels.

To finish off your doors, I find thin plastic such as micro strip is ideal for representing any metal rubbing plates, exposed hinges and letterboxes. Flat-topped dressmaking pins are just the job

**9.** A typical pair of boarded doors.

**10.** This pair of doors features decorative glazing.

**11.** Modern doors – Ok who can't spell (pronunciation is right though!).

**12.** This Door at Downham Market on the GER is flanked by matching glazed screens.

for rounded doorknobs, whereas pins with larger heads can be easily filed down to represent lever handles. If you need to make door handles and the old fashioned type of thumb operated door latch, take some thin brass wire and bend it into a staple shape using a pair of fine pliers. The tip of another length of wire can then be flattened to represent the thumb press. Wherever you have door furniture, you will need to drill small holes through the plastic door with a small drill held in a pin vice to fit them and it is best to secure the metal parts in place using a spot of superglue.

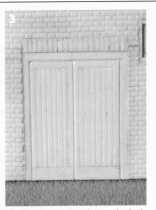

**1.** Door frames are made in the same manner as windows.

**2.** A simple scribed boarded door.

**3.** This frame door has a planked infill.

**4.** A completed simple door with a pin head door knob.

**5.** This door is made using both plastic sheet and micro strip.

**6.** A simple scribed panelled door.

**7.** Proprietary doors can also be used.

**8.** This door has a home made latch.

This large timber shed, based on a prototype from Moreton-in-Marsh features an unusual curved roof.

Assuming that you have taken the trouble to plan your model properly and have built all of the walls to the correct dimensions, the assembly process should be extremely straightforward indeed. Whether modelling a complicated structure with several wings or merely a simple rectangular box it is a good idea to always follow the same standard order of construction. Having photographed my model, based on the ex-GNR station building at Wansford Road near Peterborough, I think it will be useful to use this as a pictorial guide and follow its progress stage-by-stage as the various components are fitted together. After this we will take a look at various types of roof structure and will see how something a little out of the ordinary, in the shape of a curved roof, can be scratch-built.

## Assembly Of The Walls

The best place to start the assembly process off is at any corner of the building by simply fixing one of the end walls to a longer main wall. If at first you are not too confident, a useful tip if just starting out is to attempt one of the back corners that will be hidden from view on the completed model first. Then, once you have successfully finished a couple of joints, make your way gradually around to the front. During this, and for that matter at all subsequent stages of

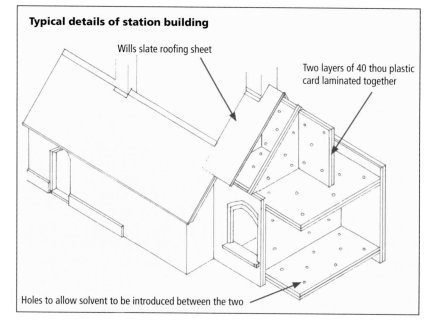

**Typical details of station building**

Wills slate roofing sheet

Two layers of 40 thou plastic card laminated together

Holes to allow solvent to be introduced between the two

the assembly process, it is essential that you make one hundred percent certain that the walls being fixed together are both at right angles to each other and are perfectly plumb vertically to the base. To help with this I always check the angles with the aid of a small engineer's square.

As you can see from the photos, I avoid the time consuming process of mitring these joints wherever possible by forming a rebate on the main elevation by simply stopping the backing sheet short of the end of the wall. The end wall then fits snugly into the rebate where it can be glued in place without the two sections slipping or moving around. I always make sure that I use a reasonable amount of solvent along these joints and ensure that enough pressure is applied to squeeze out a little excess soft plastic from the line of the joint. I know this may look a mess at the time but the liquefied plastic actually acts as filler and, having been left for a week or so to harden and can then be filed perfectly smooth. To complete the job the stone courses are then quickly carried round the corners using the scraperboard tool or the tip of a sharp knife.

Having let the first stage harden for a while, it is now time to add a section of the floor and the first dividing wall that will eventually add considerable strength and rigidity to the structure. You will see from the photos that I find it useful to make tiny spacers out of plastic strip that are located and stuck to the walls prior to assembly. This simple tip will not only ensure that the floor is correctly positioned in relation to the walls, but will make the parts much easier to hold together as the solvent dries out. Once the first section has been firmly fixed in place, more floor and wall sections can be added in sequence until you are ready to add the remaining outer walls. The key tip here is always to remember to let the solvent harden between jobs; after all the last thing you want is for the whole structure to collapse like a stack of playing cards.

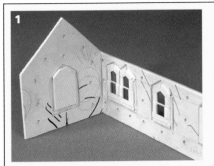

**1.** Starting at one end, the first two wall sections are brought together.

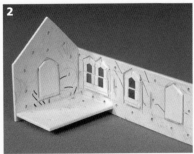

**2.** A floor section stiffens the embryonic structure and locates the first division.

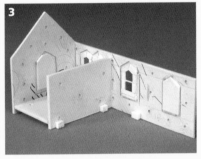

**3.** With the first dividing wall added, small blocks of plastic are added to locate adjoining components.

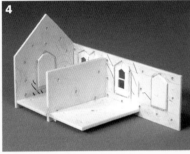

**4.** By repeating the process, you will have a core to support the remaining walls and roof base.

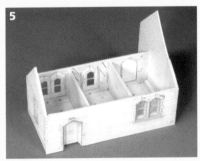

**5.** The other two walls complete the basic box of the first wing.

**6.** A sub-roof is added to provide a level base for the roof structure.

**7.** The next step is to fix in place a vertical spine that will keep the end walls in position and strengthen the completed structure.

**8.** Triangular shaped pieces are next positioned ready to support the roof slopes.

**9.** A typical corner detail.

to 5mm x 5mm in section.

On occasions where you have the need to reinforce a longer than normal span, like the top of the station's central section, try using long lengths of square section plastic glued inside. As you can see from the illustration I often use cheap and cheerful clothes pegs to hold things in place while the glue dries.

## Roof Structure

With the external walls in place, the box can finally be completed by the addition of a false ceiling that will later support the whole roof structure (unless of course your model has a flat roof in which case it will be ready for the finish to be applied). Being a creature of habit, I usually make all of the floors, strengthening partitions, false ceilings and roof supports from, yes you've guessed, two layers of 40 thou plastic card laminated back-to-back with 'Mek Pak' solvent. Don't be put off by thinking that this means twice as many

If you need to add extra strength to a corner joint or if you haven't got a square to check that the adjoining walls are square, try sticking a length of square section plastic along the edge of one of the walls before joining it to its neighbour. I tend to keep a selection of various sized manufactured sections in stock and would, in this instance, probably use a piece something close

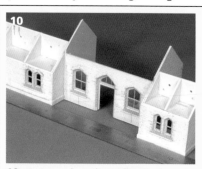

**10.** Having made up the smaller wing in much the same way, the two are brought together by the front wall of the booking office. The steel rule is a good way to ensure that the structure is in alignment.

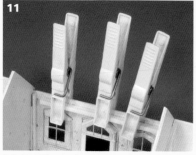

**11.** To stiffen up the centre section, a strip of sturdy plastic is cemented in place above the windows.

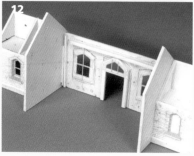

**12.** Once hardened, the structure awaits further strengthening.

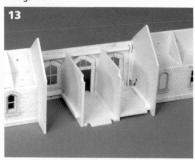

**13.** In exactly the same way as the first wing, floors and divisions are added.

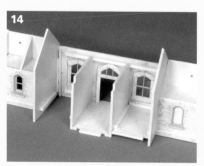

**14.** Note the sturdy plastic strengthening strips.

**15.** A touch of black paint will prevent any unwanted white plastic showing through the windows of the completed model.

parts have to be cut out, I cheat! Well, I prefer to only cut out one of the two layers accurately. The other is simply cut out using the first as a template having already been laminated to another sheet of plastic card. As elsewhere, I drill a load of small holes in the upper layer to enable the solvent to reach the lower layer fully bonding the two together in so doing.

When assembling 'box' structures like these, it is very important that you should also drill some holes through both layers of plastic to make what effectively are breathing holes. These will enable any solvent trapped inside the structure by the assembly process to evaporate and escape. If you don't vent the model you may end up with residual pockets of solvent in vapour form that may, over a period of time, attack the inner surface of the plastic sheet causing it to distort and affect the stability of the finished model.

To brace and support the roof covering it is very easy to make a simple framework, once again from two layers of 40 thou plastic card, that can be fixed to the flat upper surface of the box. To do this, firstly start by making a vertical member that runs the length of the roof under the line of the ridge and then add a series of triangular shaped pieces, similar to rafters, that can either directly support a rigid roof sheet, as is the case of using Wills roofing, or alternatively, in the case of most other roof coverings, to support a sub-roof comprised of laminated plastic card.

The only possible problem that could arise here is if you don't compensate

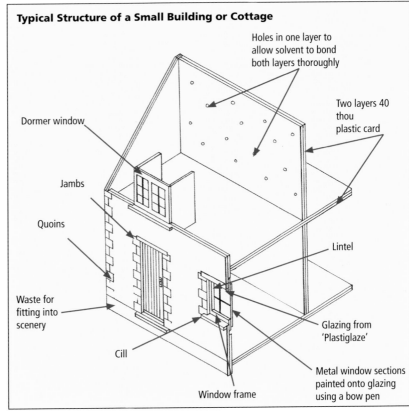

**Typical Structure of a Small Building or Cottage**

Holes in one layer to allow solvent to bond both layers thoroughly

Two layers 40 thou plastic card

Dormer window

Jambs

Quoins

Lintel

Waste for fitting into scenery

Glazing from 'Plastiglaze'

Cill

Metal window sections painted onto glazing using a bow pen

Window frame

properly for the thickness of the roof covering. If you are unsure how to do this try drawing out a cross-section of the roof to scale on a scrap of paper and the true dimensions of the triangular supports will soon become clear. Another thing to remember if you are making a thatched cottage is that the sub-roof needs to be much lower than the actual roof slope. In practice I find that the plastic card slope needs to be fixed about 5mm below the top edge of the plastic walls to allow for the thickness of the overlying thatch.

## Hipped Roofs

When you have to make a hipped roof the following tips will hopefully help you make light work of things. Firstly start with a flat sheet of plain 40thou plastic and mark it out as in the accompanying sketch. Next carefully cut out both roof slopes as shown but only scribe, not cut, along the ridge position for the time being. For reasons that will become clear in a few moments, retain the two triangles cut from the ends of the sheet and set them to one side for the time being.

**16-18.** These three photos show how the sub-roof on a thatched cottage is set lower to compensate for the thickness of the applied thatch.

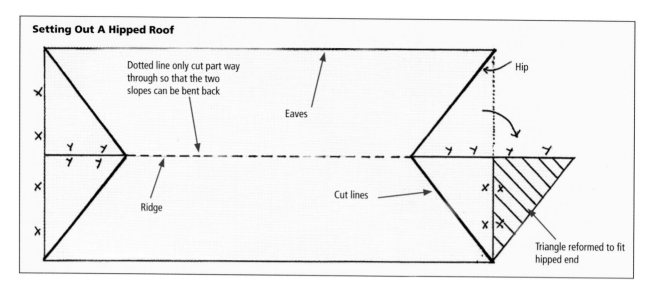

**Setting Out A Hipped Roof**

Dotted line only cut part way through so that the two slopes can be bent back

Eaves

Hip

Ridge

Cut lines

Triangle reformed to fit hipped end

Now, carefully cut about halfway through the ridge so that the two slopes can be bent back into something like their final position, but without them falling apart.

You will now see that the top edge has a groove or rebate running along it. If you hold the two slopes to roughly the correct angle apart and glue in strips of scrap plastic into the groove you can quite easily set the roof and make the ridge joint rigid at the same time. I usually fix a couple of short lengths first, checking the roof for the correct pitch and alignment, then set it aside to harden for a while before adding more strips to complete the ridge's reinforcement. Don't worry about the protruding bits of scrap plastic as these are easily filed away once the roof structure is complete.

The next part of the strengthening process is to add a second thickness of 40thou plastic to the underside of the two roof slopes. These are cut about 5mm narrower than the actual roof size in order to leave a step and a thinner, more sightly, strip around the eaves where it is visible. Then stick the two layers together and, once dry, use the upper layer as a template for cutting out the lower one. These slopes will now be able to sit on the triangular rafters that have been made as we have seen earlier.

Remember those two scrap triangles? Well we need them now. According to some sort of geometrical rule the area of any three-dimensional hipped roof slope is identical to that of it laid flat (Don't ask me why, I just picked up the fact while learning to measure roof areas years ago during my studies). If this is so, the triangle cut from the flat sheet should fit in the gap left on the end of the roof. Try it; it doesn't fit! (Unless all of the sides are the same size). Now cut the triangle into two pieces as shown, reposition them to make a slightly different shaped triangle and add a backing layer of the same material. 'Hey Presto', as if by magic (well geometry), the new part fits! Once again trim the edges to a 45° angle and stick the two ends in place, filling in any small gaps in the assembly with more scraps of waste plastic that can be trimmed down when set hard. With a backing layer added, the roof structure is complete and ready for its covering.

## Curved Roofs

Having looked at how to build the most common types of roof structure it is well worth considering the plan of attack for something a little different. Curved roofs can be anything from a simple arc to semi-circular in shape but the way they are made in model form is exactly the same. As you can see from the photos, cutting the curved

top to the walls and roof supports is a lot simpler than you might at first suppose. Having marked the centre of the curve on the 40 thou thick plastic card wall, all you have to do is to scribe a line on to the top edge using a pair of dividers. If you haven't got the proper tool, a scriber or sharp pointed nail held in an old pair of compasses will do the job equally as well. Don't press too hard while scribing, take your time and after several stokes the line will be marked to about half the thickness of the 40thou sheet. Although the plastic sheet should snap to this line if you are careful, I prefer to run the tip of a sharp knife around the groove, releasing the part in so doing. Once cleaned up, this layer can be bonded to a second thickening layer of 40thou plastic. Having then allowed the two sheets to firmly adhere it is simplicity itself to use the curved top sheet as a template to cut around ensuring that the bottom one becomes exactly the same size as the first.

If you run through the accompanying progression of photos you will see that the main assembly process is not particularly awkward at all. To form the basic shell I find it best, in the time honoured tradition, to start by gluing together one side wall and end wall and then move around the building corner by corner until all four walls are in place and the structure is beginning to take shape. As we have seen previously, always use an engineer's square to check that the corners are true and, wherever possible, add solid strips of square section polystyrene to reinforce and stiffen the joints.

Having left the shell to harden for a while, the next job is to add the curved strengthening pieces-cum-roof formers. As these have to be nicely in line, you will see from the photo that a steel ruler can be used to ensure that all is perfectly aligned before finally introducing the solvent to the joint.

The roof slopes, or should I say curves in this case, comprise once again two layers of plastic card being curved and, in a departure from my standard, are made separately from 30 thou sheet not 40 thou. In order to make the sheets more pliable and easier to fix you need to first cut the plastic sheet a bit larger than is needed and then carefully plunge it into boiling water. Once it has been given a few seconds to soften it will be flexible enough to bend round roughly to the desired curve in your fingers. By the time it has cooled down enough to become rigid again, it will be ready to be offered up to the roof formers where you can check that it is roughly the right curvature. If it isn't, simply repeat the softening process a time or two until it is a perfect fit.

Being slightly oversized the first sheet can be glued in place with 'Mek Pak', left to harden and then finally trimmed to the exact size of the roof without the need for any clever calculations and marking out. Ok, so this is another scratch-builder's dodge, but why make a simple job harder than it needs to be? When this has been done, repeat the process by adding a second strengthening layer in much the same manner as the first.

Now that we have considered how the basic structure of a model building can be formed, it is probably a good time to have a look at some of the more common types of roof covering that can be applied to it.

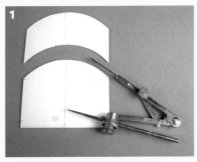

**1.** A simple scriber like this can be used to cut out the formers for the curved roof.

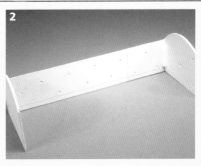

**2.** Assembly begins - three wall sections are stuck together.

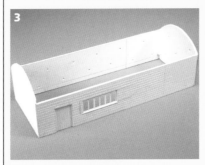

**3.** The fourth main wall is located.

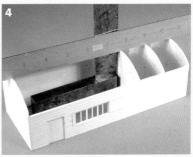

**4.** The first couple of roof supports are added, checking in so doing that everything is true and square.

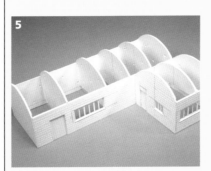

**5.** Remaining roof supports are now in place.

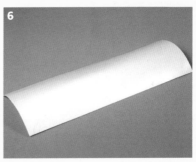

**6.** A sheet of plastic card has been pre-formed in hot water for the roof.

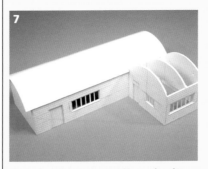

**7.** The first slightly over-sized layer of roof is fixed on, but is yet to be trimmed.

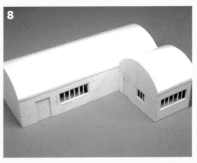

**8.** A second layer is added to both wings of the building.

This row of thatched cottages features easy to make brick chimney stacks.

Before we take a look at how to build a basic chimney stack there are a couple of simple rules of thumb that should, in most instances, help you keep things pretty much in proportion with the prototype. Firstly, if a chimney stack is positioned on the ridge of a building, the minimum height from the top of the chimney pot to the ridge line needs to be 600mm in real life. Similarly if the stack is within 600mm either side of the ridge, the top of the chimney needs to be roughly the same height above the ridge line as if it were on top of the ridge itself (ie: it would be slightly longer). Where a chimney stack passes a roof, but is more than 600mm away from the ridge, then the total height need only be about 1000mm.

**1.** A very basic brick chimney.

**2.** An ornate Midland Railway brick chimney.

**3.** A tall double brick chimney with modern pots.

All of these are really to allow for the wind pressures that act on the roof and affect the draughting of the fire below, but still need to be incorporated to make a model look just right.

Chimney pots also need to be given a little thought so don't forget to photograph them when you are surveying your prototype. I know it is probably one of my pet hates but I have, in the past, seen many a smashing building ruined by tiny undersized chimney pots with such small bores that they would never act as an effective flue in real life. In reality the minimum flue diameter would be around 9", that's 3mm in 4mm scale. The style of pot adopted is, as you would expect, largely down to the preference of individual architects and railway companies, some pots used particularly in the Victorian era, were very ornate indeed and often featured unusual shaped cowls and grilles to aid the effectiveness of its flue. Indeed the height and design of chimney pots varies so much that you could almost fill a book on the topic.

## A Simple Chimney Stack

To make a basic brick chimney stack, start by cutting out several strips of Slater's embossed brick plastic card for the front, back and sides of the stack. As you are doing this, always ensure that the vertical joints line up with the nearest brick or half brick indentations of the embossed sheet. Don't worry too much about getting the length spot on as we can trim the chimney to length later. Next take one of the strips, long enough for both sides of the chimney, and fully bond

**4.** Brick and stone combine on Wansford's LNWR building.

**5.** A typical decorative stone chimney.

**6.** This is a double flued stone version.

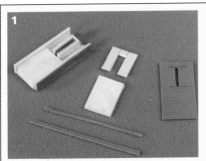

**7.** Downham Market station's brick chimneys.

**8.** This stone chimney literally does crown the roof.

**9.** Finely detailed brick chimney at Blickling Hall.

it to a piece of 40thou plastic card using a reasonable amount of solvent. When this has had time to harden, cut around the embossed layer and cut to length, ending up with a pair of laminated chimney wall sections. I normally rub the edges of these parts with a large file, to make sure they are perfectly straight and square in preparation for assembly. Now neatly bond one of the embossed front/back walls to the laminated side wall, keeping the brick courses in alignment on the adjacent components as you do so. Don't forget to check that the walls are still at right angles with the engineer's square before repeating the exercise with the

**1.** The components of a brick chimney.

**2.** This chimney is set within a scribed stone surround.

**3.** The completed chimney awaits painting.

other two walls. At this point, set both sub-assemblies aside for a while to allow them to dry and harden.

Again, while checking for squareness and alignment of the courses, take the two components and offer them together to form a box section. If you are happy with the fit, run some solvent into the joints and hold the parts together for a few minutes until the glue starts to harden. If the parts are not true to each other they may need a little further fettling with a file until they are.

At this point I always find it best to fill the central void with specially cut strips of plastic card of varying thicknesses until you end up with a solid laminated stack. As you can see from my sketch, I prefer, wherever possible, to make my chimney stacks straddle the spine of the roof or, where offset from the ridge, a rafter bracing. This not only makes the chimney easier to assemble, but also allows adjustment both side-to-side and up-and-down when finally fixing into position on the model. If your chimney is of solid brickwork and isn't capped by a pot, simply finish the laminated infill about 10mm or so below the top of the chimney so it doesn't show on the completed model.

Now we have a basic chimney stack, it is a very easy task to cut out more pieces of embossed brickwork and add them to represent any decorative thickenings, bands and corbelling that may be part of the prototype. I always make overlapping corner joints rather than mitred ones, largely because when set solid they can be filed flush and the mortar courses missing on the ends of exposed plastic parts can be reinstated using a craft knife. To cap the structure, take a piece of 40 thou plastic card and file away the edges to represent the mortar haunching that surrounds the chimney pots and keeps them in place. As most commercially available chimney pots have some kind of peg for fixing, a hole or holes need to be drilled vertically on the centre line of the stack. With such a diverse range of chimney pot designs found on various

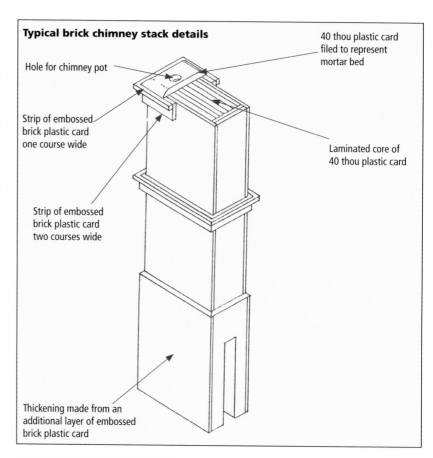

**Typical brick chimney stack details**

Hole for chimney pot

40 thou plastic card filed to represent mortar bed

Strip of embossed brick plastic card one course wide

Laminated core of 40 thou plastic card

Strip of embossed brick plastic card two courses wide

Thickening made from an additional layer of embossed brick plastic card

**1.** A simple brick-built chimney stack.

**2.** Decorative brickwork features on this chimney stack.

**3.** This scribed stone chimney stack has turned brass pots.

**4.** Clay baffles act as an alternative to a chimney pot.

**1.** The scribed stone parts are firstly laminated together.

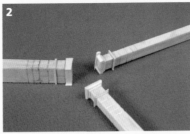

**2.** Several layers of strip form the detailing.

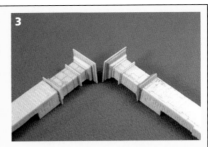

**3.** Milliput is added to make weathered or sloping stones.

**4.** The chimney stack is then fixed to the main walls.

**5.** The completed chimney with ornate baffles added.

types of buildings, it is probably simplest to fit some of the excellent examples available in white metal from firms such as Langley or Scalelink. If you have access to a small lathe you can, of course, turn some up from brass especially for the job in hand.

Stone chimney stacks are, not surprisingly, best built in pretty much the same way as brick ones, with the embossed brick coverings being substituted by scribed plastic card ones. When I was making the rather ornate ones for my station building, I had to experiment with ways to create some quite complicated curved stone embellishments. In the end I came up with a method combining my favoured plastic strips and sections with the addition of small amounts of 'Milliput' modelling putty to achieve the desired effect.

When you have to make a large square section industrial brick chimney, like the one I made for the creamery at Moreton-in-Marsh, it is probably best to make then from embossed plastic card facing as normal but with a couple of layers of 40 thou backing to each wall. This will not only stiffen up the structure nicely but will prototypically leave the top open as well.

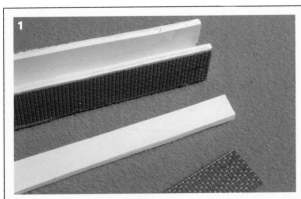

**1.** The components of a factory chimney.

**2.** The chimney nears completion.

W ansford Road station, adjacent to the A47, was on the Stamford & Essendine Railway's 1865 extension from Stamford East to join with the LNWR at Wansford (now the home of the Nene Valley Railway) at Stibbington on the A1.

Latterly run by the GNR and LNER until the closure of passenger services in 1929 and the withdrawal of goods traffic in 1931, the station still survives along with its handed twin at nearby Barnack. Both buildings have now been converted to domestic use.

With some smashing stone detailing and a reasonably simple track plan I decided to replicate both the building and track layout in 4mm scale, EM gauge, alongside my fictitious village of Paston Ridings.

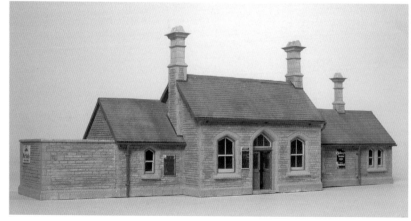

A rear view of the model.

These views are of Barnack Station which is a handed version of Wansford Road.

The front elevation.

The Bluebell Inn at Dogsthorpe in Peterborough.

As many of our lineside buildings were constructed in the style typical of the Victorian era, slates are perhaps the most common type of roof covering found on the older buildings that can be seen alongside our railways. For the model maker there are several ways that these can be reproduced to scale. The most common ones are:

• Injection moulded slates such as those manufactured by Wills.

• Purpose made paper slates made from graph or watercolour paper.

• Embossed plastic card slate strips.

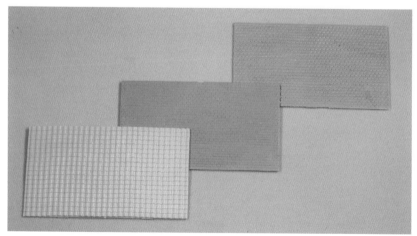

A selection of Wills roofing slates and tiles.

• Pre-coloured, printed 'brick paper' and embossed card slates.

## Wills Slates

If you have a simple small slate roof to make these sheets will certainly save you a lot of time and effort. If you look at the signal box featured in 'First Steps in Scratch-Building' in my earlier book *Lineside Buildings* from the same publisher, you will see just what I mean. The one real disadvantage of this product is that it comes in 130mm long x 75mm wide sheets that are just that little bit too small for most models and would appear, at a first glance, to be very difficult to join together without that tell tale seam being visible across some slates.

With its three relatively small sections, the station building illustrated here was suitably sized for these slate sheets but meant that the adjoining sections would have to be joined in two places. Now I know that many modellers say that is not possible, but I thought that I would have a go anyway.

The solution was one of careful planning and marking out, such that the neighbouring sheets could be joined both horizontally and vertically along the exact lines of the embossed slate courses. The fact that these joints were staggered and not the full height of the sheets helped matters a lot, as less tidying up was necessary. As you can see from the photos, the horizontal joints are not really noticeable so long as they are in alignment, but alternate vertical slates have to be filled so that they do not appear to have been cut. To do this I made up a slurry of plastic shavings, taken from the same sheets, mixed to a paste with plenty of liquid solvent. This home made filler was then pressed firmly into the unwanted joints and left to dry until it was completely solid when the resulting surface could be filed and sanded flat.

The only other thing that you need

**1.** A typical slate roof.

**2.** Large slates laid in a diamond pattern.

**3.** Decorative scallop shaped slates.

**4.** Slates are used here on a mansard roof.

to do with the Wills product is to file away and thin down the back face of the bottom edge of each sheet so that you end up with a much finer, and in my opinion much neater, appearance at the eaves.

A completed roof using Wills slates.

**1.** In its simplest form sheets of slates are cut out and fixed in place.

**2.** In this case rebates are cut in preparation for joining three sheets together.

**3.** The joint is made and filled with softened plastic prior to filling.

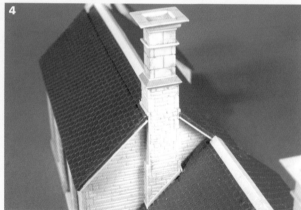

**4.** The ridges and flashings are added.

## Paper or Card Slates

I used to represent slate roofing by taking a sheet of graph paper and cutting every second or third vertical approximately 1.5mm upwards along the bottom, trimmed edge, until I ended up with a whole row so treated. The row of slates was then released by cutting along the third horizontal row up. Nowadays, being hopefully a little more discerning, I prefer to use artist's watercolour paper for its much better textured appearance.

To start with, put a sheet of paper on a drawing board or flat surface and lightly pencil in a grid of levels (see sketch). Then take the sheet and, using a sharp craft knife and a steel straight edge, trim off the bottom edge and start cutting the verticals between adjoining slates, making sure that you only go about two thirds of the way up the strip. When you have completed a whole row, a second horizontal cut will release the strip of slates and you can start the process all over again to make the next strip.

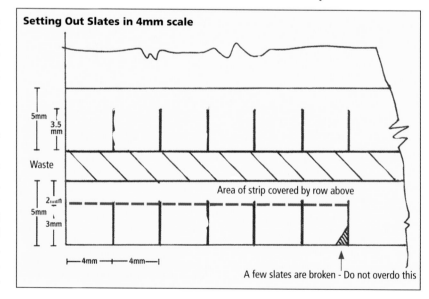

**Setting Out Slates in 4mm scale**

5mm
3.5 mm

Waste

5mm
2mm
3mm

Area of strip covered by row above

4mm — 4mm

A few slates are broken - Do not overdo this

With sufficient rows prepared and ready to play with, start by sticking the bottom one onto the plastic roof base with solvent. Although the solvent makes the plastic surface tacky enough to fix the slates in place, I find that each of the bottom edges (where paper overlies paper) of subsequent overlapping rows will benefit from the application of a very fine line of PVA glue before it is positioned. When you are happy that it is in alignment, with joints neatly staggered, press it down and fix the upper edge, where paper once again hits the surface of the plastic roof, with solvent. By using two types of adhesive both paper-to-paper and paper-to-plastic card joints are made firm, ensuring that the slates cannot lift due to damp or handling at some point in the future. Once the whole roof has been covered in this manner, trim away the excess material with a sharp knife, then you are ready to finish things off with the ridge and hip tiles.

Several variations on this general theme exist. I have for example, seen some modellers making two cuts between adjacent slates to accentuate the joints or snip off lots of tiles to give a more random effect. This is great for an old run-down structure but I do not personally feel that the gap should be too pronounced, and that we shouldn't over accentuate dilapidation, particularly as slates in real life need to be closely butt jointed together to keep out the rain and the weather.

Other model makers mark their slates out on sheets of artist's paper in much the same way as described above, but wash them with streaks of water colour before fixing in place. When they are eventually mounted on the model they end up with very random but marked contrasting coloured effect. I will admit that I have occasionally seen slate roofs with a large variation in colour but it is more likely that any changes in tone would be much more subtle across the roof. In practice, slates for a building would be bought in one batch from the same quarry to ensure that the finished

A typical roof covered with slates cut from artist's watercolour paper.

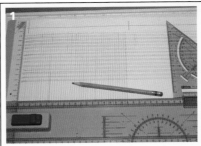

**1.** The slates are marked out prior to cutting.

**2.** The next step is to cut the verticals between individual slates.

**3.** A vertical cut releases rows of slates ready to use.

**4.** The first layer is stuck down to the roof slope.

**5.** A second layer is added above the first.

**6.** The process continues until the roof is covered.

**7.** The verges are trimmed once the roof has been covered.

**8.** A simple paper ridge is added at the apex of the roof.

**9.** The final task is to paint and weather the roof.

roof has a reasonably uniform appearance. Exceptions to this rule always occur such as when a roof has been patch repaired or when an extension or wing of a property has been added at a later time. In any case, weathering of slate roofs tends to take on a more streaked appearance which, in my opinion, is best done once the whole roof has been completed.

## Embossed Plastic Card Slates

Embossed plastic card slate strips can be cut out and fixed in a similar way to that used with the paper method. If anything I find that this material is perhaps a little too coarse for the job, largely as the product is somewhat thicker than it should be in scale.

## Printed Slates

Pre-coloured printed card slates come in three basic varieties. The first are flat printed sheets with no relief whatsoever and are identical to those found in many basic card kits. Being pretty unconvincing, I would tend not to use these at all.

Some types of brick paper can be cut into strips and laid over each other in rows just as we have seen with the paper method. Providing that they have a matt finish, these can look pretty effective, but can be spoilt by a white edge at the bottom of each row where the paper sheet has been trimmed to size. Perhaps I have never seen the logic in paying for a printed version that can be bettered for just a few pence spent on a sheet of paper.

Finally, although I have seen embossed sheets marketed in the past,

This simple row of cottages features a layered roof of watercolour paper slates.

I have discounted them for use, largely as I have found them a little too coarse in most instances.

## STONE ROOFS
### Natural Stone Slates

In some parts of the country, the Cotswolds for example, almost all of the older buildings, and a lot of the newer ones for that matter, are covered in slates made from local stone. Slates, such as those from Collyweston, are somewhat thicker than their more common cousins, have a natural stone colour and texture, and in most instances are laid up the roof in diminishing width courses.

To model these, it is possible to modify the basic paper strip method used for slates using a thin card instead of watercolour paper. If the type of slate you need has a more uneven, textured surface, try using thin plastic card strips, which can be scribed and shaved with a sharp knife before fixing. If not, pre-textured wet-and-dry paper also looks quite good. With courses diminishing one on top of another, it is essential that you plan your roof very carefully indeed, so that courses on opposite and adjoining roof slopes tie in faultlessly. Always draw to scale and plan the way that you are going to reduce the width of the slate strips, and the way that they are to be set out, on a scrap of paper before you begin. I know that we all want to get started

With Collyweston stoned slates, the courses become narrower as you move up the roof towards the ridge.

in a fit of enthusiasm, but believe me from experience; a few extra minutes in the planning stage always pays off in the end.

## TILED ROOFS

Unlike slates that are quarried from natural material, tiles are man-made from clay, concrete and in the past asbestos cement. More recently, in an attempt to find a cheaper alternative to some of the traditional types of roofing, materials such as fibreglass and stamped metal have started to be used.

## Plain Clay or Concrete Tiles and Asbestos Cement Tiles

Whichever method you adopt, it is useful to know that plain concrete or clay tiles can be represented in exactly the same way as slates. Although these types of tile are manufactured from different materials, the only difference from the modeller's perspective is in the colour that the roof is painted on completion. Once again sizes do vary so always check the prototype if you can before starting work.

**1.** Plain tiles can be made in exactly the same way as slates.

**2.** This dilapidated plain tile roof has much modelling potential!

## Clay or Concrete Pan Tiles

Now although I have seen some very creditable but painstaking efforts at handmaking individual tiles, where modellers have made up individual card pantiles on a jig and stuck them onto a roof one at a time, I tend to fight shy of making my own pantiles and really feel that the only sane option here is to use the Wills injection moulded sheets. As with slates, you still have the disadvantage of a relatively small sheet size, but as the 'pans' fit above each other down the roof and are not staggered as with slates, both the top and sides of sheets can be joined together much more easily. Once again a little work with a rat-tailed file on the lower edge of each sheet will reap dividends, as the profile of the tiles at the eaves will quickly be revealed. This process may take a few

**1.** A pantiled roof.

**2.** Tiles with a corrugated finish and decorative tile ridge.

**3.** Modern interlocking roofing tiles.

**4.** A close up of a pantile roof showing the vertical joints.

TOP LEFT: Rounded ridge and hip tiles on Market Bosworth station roof.
TOP RIGHT: Lead ridges and hips on Welwyn North Station.

BOTTOM LEFT: An angular hip tile with raised joints.
BOTTOM RIGHT: This spire has plain hip tiles.

**1.** An angular ridge with raised joints in model form.

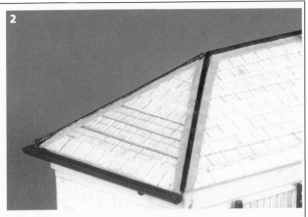

**2.** This ridge is easily made with thick paper and plastic rod.

minutes to do but believe me is really worth the extra effort.

## Ridge and Hip Tiles

Irrespective of whether you have a tiled or slated roof, all ridges and hips need to be covered with a row of purpose made tiles. The most common types tend to be either half round, or simply vee-shaped, but countless more decorative examples also exist that may need a little more thought in modelling.

Where you have a half round ridge the best method, I find, is to simply cut plastic strip of the correct section to length or, as I have done in the past, file up some brass tube to the correct profile using the gutter-making jig that you will see later.

The station at Shipston-on-Stour featured a tile with a rounded section along the line of the ridge (or hip), and a flat part on either side, that covers the top layers of slating on either side. To represent these, simply cut a length of plastic rod to size and glue it along the intersection between the two roof slopes.

For the flat sections of tile, carefully cut some strips of brown paper from an old envelope and fix them in place on either side of the rod. With a little careful trimming at the joints between adjoining sections, the job is a lot less awkward than you may at first think.

For a vee-shaped ridge, you can crown the apex of the two slopes using two strips of plastic card glued together on top of the slate roof. If, as with my signal box, the ridge has decorative raised joints, small lengths of 10 thou x 20 thou plastic strip can soon be added to represent the detail found on the prototype.

## Flashings

Where all except thatched roof coverings abut a brick wall or chimney they need to be flashed to prevent water penetration through the joint. Traditionally this has been done by using lead sheeting that is dressed both up from the roofing and down over the upstanding flashing from the abutting wall. From the modellers perspective all that we see is a strip or band of leadwork at the junction of the two materials. Having tried various methods I find that thin strips of plastic card trimmed to shape are the best way of representing flashings. The only difficult, or rather fiddly, task here is when you have to model a flashing of the stepped variety that needs to be cut neatly to shape and profile.

**1.** Typical flashings to the base of a brick chimney stack.

**2.** A stepped lead flashing where a roof abuts a wall.

**3.** A lead valley at Wells GER station.

**4.** Flashings to an abutment above a rainwater hopper.

Shipston on Stour's goods shed is an interesting structure with both corrugated walls and roof.

Although now pretty much displaced by the use of modern plastic coated steel profile sheeting, there was a time when corrugated iron was the first choice covering for almost any lightweight industrial roof, shed or warehouse. Together with its asbestos cement cousin, these materials were widely used right up until the 1960s. Being cheap and readily available, corrugated iron was also widely used to make lean-to roofs on cottage extensions and, as I have seen many times in the Fens, was also put to use in re-roofing whole run down buildings that could not presumably afford a new thatched or tiled roof.

Despite several moulded plastic alternatives being available on the market, I still prefer to use the aluminium 'Eastwell Ironworks' products marketed in both 4mm and 7mm scales by Ambis Engineering of Ilford.

**1.** A typical corrugated iron roof.

**2.** Corrugated asbestos cement sheeting.

**3.** This industrial roof has both rooflights and ventilators.

**4.** Modern roofs and walls have a flat corrugated profile.

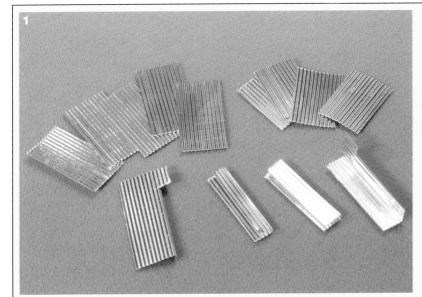

**1.** Various cut pieces of corrugated aluminium sheet.

**2.** A simple roof covered in sheeting.

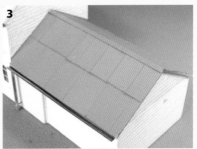

**3.** A coat of spray car primer prepares the surface for painting.

**4.** The aluminium sheets are easily curved around a former.

Each pack contains corrugated strips that measure 130mm long x 32mm wide, which can be easily trimmed to size using a sharp modelling knife and a steel rule without destroying the corrugations. If you wish, you can simply use long strips of the corrugated sheet with just laps at the tops of each sheet. However, it really does look a lot more realistic if you cut the strips in to individual scale-sized sheets and stick them down onto a flat plastic card or plywood base. Typically these are 8' x 4' in size (32mm x 16mm in 4mm scale) and are fixed in place with head-laps at the tops of the sheets and side-laps between adjoining ones. Being made of aluminium foil, the sheets can also be readily bent to shape and curved around a former to almost any radius.

If you decide to really go to town and make something like a part-roofed steel frame with trusses made from brass angle, you may be interested to know that Ambis also sell strips of the same profile made from copper foil, that will usefully allow you to solder the sheeting in place.

Assuming that you have already made a plastic card or plywood shell, we can now see how it is given a corrugated covering. In order to replicate the staggered joints of the prototype sheeting, you need to cut the corrugated sheets into individual 4' wide scale strips. Despite being made from metal, these sheets are extremely easy to cut to size. All you have to do is to measure and mark the line of the cut and then, using a sharp craft knife, firmly score (not cut through) the aluminium corrugations. Now here's the clever bit, fold back the sheeting along the line of the cut and the two

**5.** Sheets are stuck onto the building using contact adhesive.

**1.** Sheets can be left over size and can be trimmed in-situ if necessary.

**2.** Note the marks to ensure the rows of sheets are kept in alignment.

parts will literally fall apart. The same method works equally well both along and across the corrugations and does not normally damage the appearance of the cut edges so produced.

Where you need the corrugated sheet to fit awkward shapes, such as those around windows, or when it is bent up into flashings that wrap the angles surrounding a door, you will need to depart from the usual procedure of simply cutting and sticking. On these occasions, I find it best to cut out individual sheets to size, snip a line between the flat and bent sections of the sheet using some sharp nail scissors and then bend back the flashing around a metal straight edge such as my trusty old steel ruler. Ok, I agree that this can be a little more fiddly and time consuming, but the results are well worth it, believe me. If you have any worries here, or at any other stage of construction, don't be afraid to have a trial run. Just mess about with an odd scrap of material, practice your proposed method and things will come together in no time at all.

I prefer to stick the individual sheets to the building's carcass with 'user-friendly' solvent free 'Evo-stik'. Initially when I first made buildings of this type, I started by applying a liberal coating of adhesive to each individual cut sheet, using the tip of a small screwdriver and at the same time I treated a small area of

the walls with the same glue. Once dry to the touch, the piece of sheeting was located on the plywood wall, and after the application of a little firm pressure, the joint was complete. After a while, I became fed up with spreading glue on each tiny sheet so, in an attempt to try and speed up the process, I decided to put the glue on the back of a whole strip of corrugated aluminium before it was cut to size. To my delight, the sheet with dry adhesive cut just as well as the untreated variety and, more importantly, the glue didn't rub off in the process. With this in mind the main areas of the roof can be sheeted, leaving the openings and apertures to trim with individually

cut and fixed flashings specifically made to suit each location. Although not strictly speaking essential, I feel that it is well worthwhile to carefully place a little glue on the top edge of all sheets where others overlap them. This simple course of action, although a little messy, will in fact, prevent the edges of the aluminium sheets from lifting and becoming dog-eared during handling.

Having covered the whole roof, making sure that the layers are level, you come to the apex or ridge. These, and any other roof flashings for that matter, can be made from thin aluminium foil. To do this, cut out a piece of foil slightly larger than the

**3.** The completed goods shed ready for painting.

flashing needed and fold it in two, then mark out the width of the ridge etc. (say 2-3 mm) and cut along this line while still flat. Finally, open out the flashing to the desired angle, trim to length and glue on top of the roof.

As a result of the cutting and sticking process, no matter how carefully you apply the glue, you inevitably end up with a load of tiny glue 'snots' (now there's a technical term from the building trade), that need to be removed from the corrugations prior to completion. Being of a rubbery nature these are fairly easy to remove without damage by the careful downward action of a blunted cocktail stick along the corrugations. Only where absolutely necessary, a little light trimming using a craft knife may be needed to remove the more stubborn bits of glue. Finally a quick rub over with a fibreglass brush will prepare the corrugated sheet ready for a coat of spray car primer and subsequent painting.

## Flat Roofing

Flat roofs mainly comprise flat metal sheeting such as lead or copper, that is laid over a wooden or metal roof deck, more commonly bitumen felt (and its modern single ply successors) and asphalt. In model form the only difference is in the grittiness of the surface and, to a lesser extent the

**1.** This extension has a sheet metal flat roof.

jointing of the prototype sheets.

Roofs made from lead or copper can be made very quickly from plain sheets of plastic card as they have a nice smooth surface. The only things you have to add are the standing seam joints and upstands/labours from micro strip and thin plastic card respectively.

Flat felt roofs are quite simple to make using the same granular finish that can be applied to walls when modelling cement rendering. Initially I tried ordinary sand, but dismissed it as being far too coarse and overscale. Then, while looking for an old jar of foundry sand that I used to have in my

scenery box, I came across some aluminium oxide grit used in the Badger abrasive blasting tool this was much finer and well suited to the job in hand.

Just as we have seen for the rendered walls, the powder is scattered onto wet liquid polystyrene cement that has been spread liberally on the surface of the roof. Once it has been pressed firmly into the tacky plastic and left to dry, the excess grit is washed off and the surprisingly convincing surface will be ready for painting. When this has been completed, any upstands or dressing details can be simply added using plastic strip cut to size and glued in place.

**2.** A typical flat roof prior to the fitting of upstands from plastic strip.

**3.** The protoype for comparison.

A busy scene on Michael Warner's Shipston-on-Stour branch.

As you will have already seen in the pages of this handbook, I prefer to make the majority of my scratch-built buildings from plastic card. There are however exceptions and this is one of them. Where there is a need to span a large open area inside the model it can be advantageous to make a wooden shell or carcass that is covered with embossed plastic card, corrugated sheeting or, as in this case, a combination of the two. With no better place to start let's begin by having a look at the basic shell.

## Wooden Structure

As the wooden box that forms the main structure needs to be thin-walled but also rigid, I decided to make the walls from 2mm thick plywood that I bought from my local radio-controlled aircraft shop. Having first marked out all of the principal dimensions for each of the components on the flat plywood sheet in pencil, it was a reasonably easy exercise to cut them out with a sharp craft knife using a steel straight edge as guide. I know some people mess about with miniature fret saws and the like, but I find a few firm cuts with a sturdy knife soon does the job. As always the simplest solutions tend to be the best!

The curves to the top edges of the end walls are, however, a little more difficult to get right. Once the curve had been marked out with a pair of compasses, each part was at first cut out slightly oversize before the straight edges were trimmed to their final dimensions in the usual way. Next a light freehand cut around the curve was made slowly and steadily following the pencil mark. As the second and third passes of the knife will, I find if you are careful, follow the same cut line as the first, the excess ply is then much easier to remove. Finally, to tidy things up, all I needed to do was to give the surface of the curve a quick rub with some sandpaper until a nice smooth edge was achieved.

Being an arc, the roof initially

presents the modeller with a problem - how do I do this and what should I use? Well, there are several options available: plastic card (as used on the timber store featured elsewhere in this book) is a possibility, but fixing it to thin wooden walls is potentially problematical; card, being very flexible, will readily bend to shape; metal sheet, once passed through a set of special rollers, will provide another solution whereas the obvious choice, particularly, as I had already chosen to make plywood walls, was to make a plywood roof supported by a series of formers.

With a decision made, a supporting structure needed to be made that was completely rigid and true. As you can see from the photos, I firstly made a series of identical plywood ribs to support the sheeting in exactly the same way as the end walls. Next these were all clamped together so that three 6mm diameter locating holes could be strategically cut through them using a vertical drill. To make sure that the separated parts would be put together correctly, the bottom flat edge was clearly marked with a pen in such a way that the marks could be easily aligned

during the assembly process. With this done three lengths of 6mm timber dowelling were then threaded through each of the holes in order, whilst roughly spacing out the ribs. Having made a few minor adjustments to satisfy myself that all was well, the framework was simply stuck together using Evo-stik woodworking glue (it used to be called 'Resin W'), checking as I did, that everything was still true and square using an engineer's square.

To begin the assembly phase, one end wall and the long wall facing the yard were fixed together at right angles using wood glue and a strip of something like 5mm x 5mm square section timber. As you can see from the photograph I always stick these wooden blocks to one of the walls first and set them aside to dry before sticking on the adjoining parts. I suppose you could, if you wished, make up a corner with all three parts in one go but the wet glue is quite fluid for a while and you can end up with a joint that has slipped out of true as it sets.

The next step is to thread the dowels poking out at one end of the roof support structure through the end wall of the embryonic assembly and add the

second full width cross wall to the other. Yet again I checked all was perfectly square at this stage and glued this second end wall neatly in place. In much the same way I followed on by adding the two wall sections that form the two storey offices on one end of the building and the remaining long wall that faces the running line. Finally, to strengthen the structure and to provide a suitable surface for fixing the goods shed to the layout, I added a couple of strips of the same square timber already used on the corners to the bottom edges of the two long walls.

With all of the walls now in place it was time to add the roof. To make life simple I chose to make this from thinner 1mm plywood and decided not to attempt to cut the roof sheet exactly to size before it was fixed in place. Instead I decided to try an old dodge and cut it slightly over the finished dimensions of the roof. Being much more flexible than the ply used on the walls it was really easy to glue and clamp it in place over the ribbed framework. I started by gluing the roof along one edge and let the whole thing harden before gluing the centre section and the other edge in turn.

**1.** The principal plywood parts after cutting out.

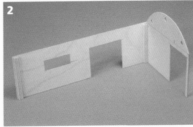

**2.** Assembly begins - note the square section timber used to reinforce the corners.

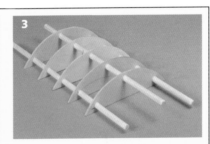

**3.** These ribs held apart by wooden dowels make a solid support to the curved roof.

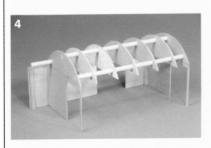

**4.** The roof supports are added to the first few walls.

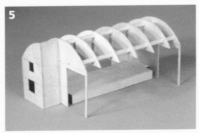

**5.** With office walls added the internal platform is tried for size.

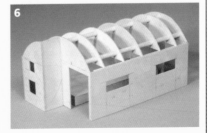

**6.** A stage further reveals the rest of the walls in position.

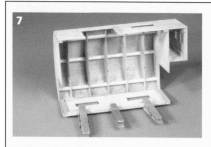

**7.** This interior view illustrates how clothes pegs can be used to clamp parts together while being glued.

**8.** Looking like a building at last. The roof covering glued in position and the waste around the edges trimmed to size.

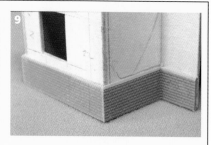

**9.** Close-up of the brick plinth around the base of the goods shed. The butt joints at the corners await cutting of the mortar joints.

**10.** The first few sheets have been positioned around one corner of the building overlapping each other just as the prototype.

**11.** Rainwater goods are fabricated from brass section.

**12.** The canopy over the yard loading door is simply made from ply, wood strip, plastic and corrugated sheeting.

When the whole sheet was in place and the glue had hardened overnight, I simply shaved away the excess wood that overhung the walls and the shell was pretty much complete

## Brick plinths

Skirting the base of the external walls is a brick plinth that rises for a couple of feet above the foundations. In reality this feature protrudes about one brick thickness from the face of the wall and has a raking top to allow easy dispersal of rainwater falling from the corrugated sheeting above. To make this I first took two layers of Slater's embossed English Bond brickwork, bonded them together and cut strips to the correct height. Next, before they could be attached to the model, the top brick course had to be carefully filed back to give the sloping effect seen on the real building. Having then cut the plinth to length, a liberal coating of Evo-stik solvent-free contact adhesive was applied to the back of the embossed plastic card strip and to the bottom couple of centimetres

or so of the wooden carcass. Once both surfaces had become dry to the touch, the two elements were brought together and the first section was in place. As you might expect the rest of the plinths were prepared, trimmed to length and added to the structure in much the same fashion.

Rather than mess about with mitred corners I simply butted the plastic-to-plastic joint together and brushed in a spot of solvent such that, under a little firm pressure, the softened plastic filled the joint between adjoining plinth wall sections. Once the plinth had been left for a few days to set hard, any excess material can be easily filed smooth and the brick courses reinstated using a knife or scriber.

## Windows

We have already seen that you don't always have to make every component of a scratch-built building and this goods shed was no exception. In this case I found some etched-brass windows made by Ambis Engineering of Ilford

dramatically eased the burden.

Although the etching's pane size was just about right, these windows actually had three panes vertically and six panes horizontally, whereas the ones I wanted were only five panes wide but set in pairs with a central dividing member between them. The solution to this predicament was to very carefully snip away one pane width from two etched windows and just as carefully file up the cut edges ready for fabrication. Next a piece of 1mm wide brass strip was cut slightly longer than the height of the finished window and was soldered between the trimmed ends of the two etchings. As the resulting assembly had very little spare frame available to allow the windows to be glued in place, I thought that it would be more practical to add a couple of wings to each window unit using scraps of sprue from the spare etchings. After a quick tidy up with a small file, the main windows were ready for fixing to the wooden shell using the same solvent-free contact adhesive as already used earlier

In the late 1980s the goods shed was in use but was by then falling into an unkempt state.
The Late Michael Warner

did quite nicely although I did notice that the corners of the sheets not overlapped by neighbouring rows were prone to a very slight lifting from the curve necessitating an additional spot of glue to rectify the situation. Once again it didn't take long to find a simple solution. All I did was to form each individual sheet around a curved surface somewhat smaller in radius than that of the finished roof (in my case a large drill chuck off my lathe was used).

Once some 169 individual corrugated parts had been painstakingly applied to the shell, the only thing left to finish off the roof was to make up some rainwater pipes and gutters from brass section and rod and fix them in place on the model.

to fix the embossed plastic card to the plywood walls.

Turning to the office end of the goods shed, there are two more windows both of an odd size and pattern to the rest. As luck would have it, I found that the lower one could be represented quite easily by one of the Ambis windows if some of the upright glazing bars were removed. The other smaller window was made by cutting away the bottom corner of a larger window (this time from the D&S range), then adding a couple of strips of spare brass sprue to reform the frame. I know all of this sounds like a lot of messing about, but at the end of the day I ended up with windows that were just about right for the prototype. Indeed, contrary to what some readers might imagine, the whole lot only took just over an hour to make!

## Roof and wall sheeting

To cover the roof I elected to once again use my favoured corrugated aluminium strips from Ambis Engineering that had been cut into individual sheets just like the real thing. Having a large curved expanse of roof to cover, the one thing I felt important was to ensure, that the individual sheets were in complete alignment both along and across the roof. To do this, I simply marked a series of dots at exactly 20mm intervals across the roof, to act as a guide and ensure that the individual rows comprised a prototypically staggered but regular pattern of standard sheets sizes. Being pretty thin, I initially simply tried to stick the tiny corrugated sheets down onto the plywood surface assuming that the strength of the contact adhesive would bring the aluminium to the curve of the roof. Well, in practice it

## Canopy, interior, doors and porch

Facing the yard is a small flat-roofed canopy. Just like the rest of the building, I made this from ply with corrugated aluminium sheeting to the sides. The canopy was then capped with a plastic card roof with matching plastic fascias around its perimeter. As I felt that the joint between the canopy and the main building was a potential problem (having to be positioned once the wall sheeting was in place and painted), a bit of thought and design work was required. In the end I decided to make up a simple fixing device consisting of a flat brass plate with a couple of lengths of brass rod soldered to it. By sticking the plate to the underside of the canopy with contact adhesive, the method of fixing would be hidden from view on the completed model. The two pins could then fit into a couple of small holes drilled in corresponding locations on the external walls of the goods shed. Some of the pictures show the internal platform that sits snugly inside the shed. Once again I fabricated this from plywood with a plastic card facing: embossed brickwork for the walls and scribed plain 40thou sheet for the platform's paving.

**13.** Scratch-built from brass strip, the porch parts are pictured prior to assembly.

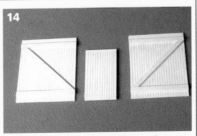

**14.** Scribed sheets of plastic sheet with rectangular strip for the bracing - the goods shed doors are ready for painting.

Rainwater pipes and gutters as seen on the cottages on Paston Ridings.

Whether connected to mains drainage, or spilling away on to an adjoining footpath or hardstanding, most buildings have some form or another of rainwater disposal system. The exception is, of course, thatch, that uses its comparatively steep roof pitch and deep projecting eaves to shed falling rainwater onto the surrounding ground below.

Traditionally gutters and rainwater pipes were made from cast iron and were fixed to the building with heavy, and sometimes ornate, brackets. In more recent times, due largely to its susceptibility to cracking, cast iron has been replaced by a host of other materials including asbestos cement, coated pressed steel, aluminium and concrete. More commonly (and especially where cost is to be kept to a minimum), plastic usually in the form of upvc is now used.

Basically two main varieties of exposed rainwater installation are widely found, namely half-round gutters with round pipes and box gutters with square section pipes. In addition, I have occasionally seen combinations of the two and also a third but less commonly used gutter section known as ogee.

As far as sizing goes, modellers do not always get things right. I have often seen models with the thinnest of wires for pipes while others have pipes as thick as pencils. Probably, and in my view, worst of all, I have spotted a lot of otherwise

**1.** Box section pipework, offset and ogee gutter.

**2.** A typical gutter to round rainwater pipe detail.

**3.** Note how the brickwork has been cut away for the pipe.

well-modelled buildings with no rainwater goods at all. Perhaps on reflection this is not so surprising, they are after all a bit fiddly to fit and are almost always the last job to get done.

In reality, to calculate the actual size of a prototype, you have to take into account a number of factors such as roof pitch, rainfall rates, gutter section, bends and the like. I am sure most modellers wouldn't have, or wouldn't even want to have, access to this information, so a modelmakers rule of thumb is needed. In essence, unless you are building a vast factory complex or a large engine shed, most gutters will be between 100mm and 150mm wide, with down-pipes ranging from 75mm to 100mm. As always, consultation of prototype photographs is well recommended, but I usually find 1mm diameter rod is about right for pipes in 4mm scale and gutters are usually between 1.5mm and 2mm wide.

For the model builder, there are a number of makes of pipes and guttering on the market, ranging from the various cast white metal varieties supplied by Scalelink to Wills' plastic ones. Having tried several varieties in the past, I find that plastic rainwater goods are very prone to damage and that white metal ones are not too easy to fix to plastic (and for that matter are also prone to being readily knocked out of shape). As a result, I now prefer to set to and scratch-build my own pipes and gutters from the wide range of brass section that is now available. Square rod and channel come in the right sizes for most scales and the rod or tube used for round rainwater pipes is very easy to get hold of. The one component I find less easy to trace (although I did find a shop selling it once) is half round brass section small enough to suit most types of guttering. With the help of a simple home-made jig, brass tube can be very quickly and easily converted to half round.

To make the jig you need two strips of 1mm thick steel sheet approximately 12mm wide. Rivet or bolt these to a 30mm wide base plate of similar material

**4.** This rectangular box hopper also shows a swan neck pipe.

**5.** A typical rainwater hopper.

**6.** The connection of a rainwater pipe to a station canopy.

**7.** A rainwater shoe on an offset rainwater pipe.

**8.** Typical upvc gutters and pipework.

**9.** A modern coated metal rainwater system.

leaving a gap between them 2.5mm - 3mm wide to take the brass rod. Don't worry too much about the workmanship, any old scrap materials will do - the completed tool will only be used for a few minutes for each length of gutter.

Now take a length of 2mm diameter brass tube and secure it in the jig's central slot using a small G-clamp. Once this has been done file away the top half

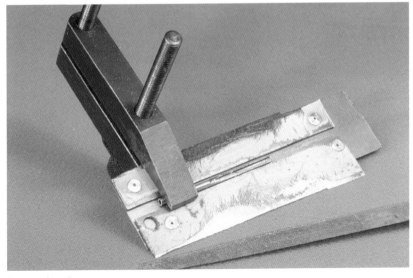

Gutter making in progress.

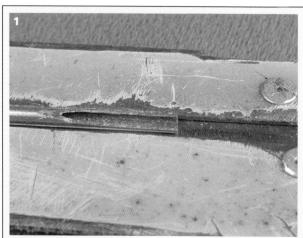

**1.** Close up of the gutter making jig.

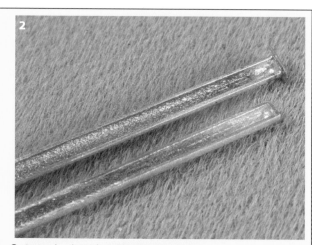

**2.** Stopped ends can be soldered to the gutters.

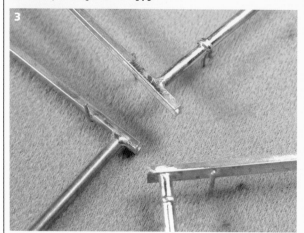

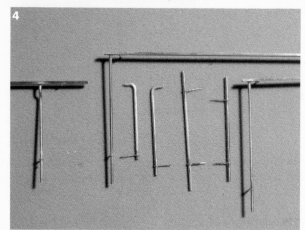

**3.** Pipes and fixings are soldered to the gutters.

**4.** A selection of rainwater and soil pipes.

of the tube making sure that the brass doesn't move or rotate. This will result in a short length of half round section. Next, undo the clamp and move the tube along, ensuring that the two upper edges of the filed length are flush with the two sides of the jig, reclamp and repeat the process as many times as it takes to manufacture the desired length.

Having cleaned away any swarf and cut the gutters to length, it is a simple job to solder a couple of brass scraps to the ends. These are filed down to shape to represent the ends. Finally, solder into position some fixing brackets made out of fine brass wire.

For the rainwater pipes, cut lengths of 1mm diameter brass rod roughly to size. If the prototype has an offset projection, (commonly known as a swan-neck), bend the top of each pipe

**5.** Gutters and rainwater pipes on a model chapel.

twice just below the point where it connects with the gutter. Check it against the model for size before finally trimming to length. Small brass split pins are then soldered at intervals along the pipe to represent the brackets commonly found on the cast iron originals. Always leave a good-sized tail of brass on the back, so that the pipes can be fixed into corresponding holes drilled in the plastic walls of the main building structure.

ABOVE: The rainwater goods are trial fitted to the model.

RIGHT: Rainwater pipes with an unusual semi-circular hopper.

I usually solder the pipes to the gutters for added strength and, as I would with any metal components, clean up and spray them with car primer, before painting them with topcoat, prior to fixing the completed installation in place on the model.

Where two or more pipes join, or indeed where a gutter discharges through a parapet wall, it is common to find a rainwater hopper acting as a collecting-device-cum-funnel. Frequently these are very ornate cast iron components, that can be represented in model form by scraps of brass, drilled, cut out, filed to shape and soldered in place on the rainwater pipe.

Although rarely seen on modern housing, due to the requirement to insulate and conceal systems, older buildings invariably possess a plethora of exposed waste carrying pipework that emerge through the external walls and drop down the side of the building to the drains and extend upward to vent away odours. In practice, I find these vary

widely from structure to structure. It is worth remembering however, that the external pipework on a very old building is often as a result of improvements during the lifetime of the property. During the period when our railways were built, luxuries such as indoor toilets and bathrooms were a feature of the more exclusive property and were definitely not for the masses. At that time, when the privy at the bottom of the garden and the tin bath hanging up on an outside wall were commonplace, mains water inside the house was, for many, still quite a new thing. Although you would

have a kitchen sink and a small waste pipe poking through the wall, usually under the kitchen window, there would often be an outside tap or pump from an underground well nearby.

As with rainwater pipes, I find the brass rod and split pin method to be the best way to faithfully replicate the exact pattern of the prototype. Typically, for those wanting another rule of thumb, the main stack pipe together with connections to toilets are 110mm in diameter, whereas connections from baths and sinks are 38mm and 32mm respectively.

**1.** Typical cast iron waste pipes on a stone building.　**2.** External upvc soil and vent pipework.

The completed creamery in position on the late Michael Warner's impressive Moreton-in-Marsh layout.

Take a train ride through the picturesque Cotswold landscape from Oxford to Worcester and you will pass through the romantically named market town of Moreton-in-Marsh. Perhaps the most imposing lineside feature that you will see from the train is the former United Dairies creamery site and the various industrial buildings that still surround it.

If you take a few minutes to delve into its past you will uncover that the main creamery building was itself upgraded sometime in the early 1930s. One early aerial shot of the station and its surroundings shows a cluster of structures on the site that differ considerably to those that exist today. Other photos taken just a couple of

years later depict what looks like a completely new creamery with a much more modern framed building complete with flat roof, white cement rendered walls and a host of large multi-paned metal windows. Closer detective work reveals that not all is at it may seem, at first. Yes, the creamery was rebuilt but only in part. The main centre section was all new, but the original boiler house and chimney remained, albeit with a new rendered wall on the railway side to match the new section. Similarly the somewhat strange shaped store set back from the platform was retained and given a bit of a makeover as it was linked in to the new structure.

Now I know some modellers will run a mile rather than attempt to

scratch-build such a complicated structure as this, but essentially the model can be broken down into four principal structural elements; the main two storey factory building forms the focus of the construction with the boilerhouse/chimney block linked to it at the Oxford end, the strangely shaped store at the Worcester end and finally a single storey extension with a small loading dock and offices facing the yard area on the opposite side to the railway.

Having roughly drawn the creamery to scale, I was able to make a simple full-sized card mock up of the model using photocopies of my drawings stuck to bits of thin card. Well! What a monster the resultant template was. It was a lot bigger than I expected measuring no less than 415mm long x 220mm high to the top of the chimney and 205mm wide overall with the single storey extension to its back. After much planning and deliberation I decided to start construction in the obvious place and so the central two-storey building started to take shape.

## Construction

As you can see the creamery was made using the same basic methods and techniques as we have already seen elsewhere. The only real difference is that there are a lot more components to make than with a less complicated structure.

With a whole load of walls, floors and strengthening bits already made up the model assembly actually started to take shape from two places at the same time. At one end construction commenced with the flat roofed single storey section and the main two-storey building following closely behind. Meanwhile assembly of the boiler house at the opposite end of the model also began.

When it came to the bit around the back I was starting to get a bit niggled. My measurements for the side wall to the offices behind the boiler house didn't quite tie up somehow with the slope of the roof to the adjacent area and I just hadn't got anywhere near enough photographic evidence to accurately build the back wall to scale. Well, there was only one thing to do! I jumped in the car and drove the hundred or so miles to Moreton-in-Marsh so that I could have a closer look for myself.

The old creamery buildings are now divided up into a number of smaller industrial units, most of which specialise in antiques and architectural salvage. Within minutes I had been able to photograph almost all of the missing details and, thanks to the then incumbent antiques business located in the main part of the creamery, was

given permission to have a look around inside, walk around the platform side and explore the lower levels of the roof. I know it sounds really, obvious but an hour or so spent surveying the prototype in some detail really does reap dividends ten times over.

As the step-by-step photos show assembly progressed stage by stage until finally the strange shaped store building was also made up and added to the ever-increasing assembly. As you can see plenty of laminated sheet bracing is also included in the design to stiffen up the structure. Needless to say I always use an engineer's square to check that the corners are true right angles and, whenever possible, add lengths of chunky plastic strip to reinforce the joints as the model takes shape.

## Windows and Doors

As decent sized windows with many regular panes are largely difficult to reproduce consistently to scale, I

always prefer to make large industrial windows, such as the metal ones found in the creamery, using etched-brass components. With this in mind, I started to search the stands at shows for something similar that could either fit the openings as bought, or if not, could be modified to do so with a little ingenuity and a soldering iron. Being very large, the main factory ones drew a blank.

Luckily, following a chat with old friend Alan Austin, who not only helps on my layout from time to time but also runs his own cottage industry supplying etchings of unusual components to the fine-scale modeller under the Ambis Engineering banner, the option to etch some windows specifically for this model became a reality. To enable Alan to generate the master for the etching firm to use, I had to draw out to scale, each of the building's windows and various types of doors in turn, as neatly as I could, showing the fenestration, the window aperture size and the border

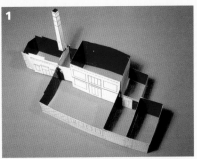

**1.** This full size cardboard mock up was used to make sure that the model was going to fit in the space available.

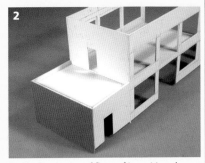

**2.** The first section of flat roof is positioned.

**3.** Plastic strip is used to stiffen the corners and to support the roof.

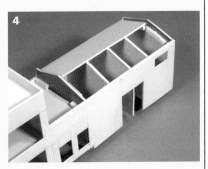

**4.** The pitched roof structure is added.

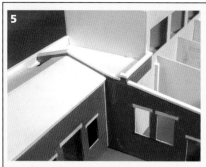

**5.** The complicated intersection between the buildings showing lintels inlaid into the embossed brickwork.

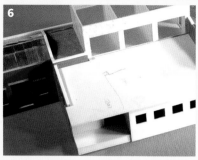

**6.** With corrugated roofs underway and flat roofs coated, the large low level roof is tried for size.

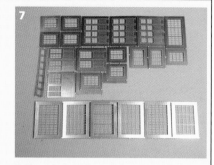

**7.** The etched windows as they arrived from Ambis.

**8.** The walls are masked to allow the metal roof to be sprayed.

**9.** Masking removed, the remainder of the store is ready for painting.

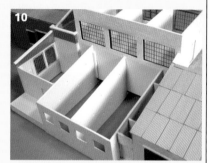

**10.** The rear of the building progresses.

**11.** A clerestory roof vent is added to the boiler house.

**12.** The canopy was made from brass sheet, brass section and old bits of rail for supports.

**13.** Painting is at an advanced stage.

around each window that would sit neatly into the rebate created in the laminated plastic walls.

When they arrived everything was an exact fit and, with only a bit of adjustment (caused by me not being able to make such wide rebates in the walls in places) they were ready to detach from the fret and use.

## Roofs & Canopy

Once again the roofs were pretty much textbook exercises to make, but the large canopy over the railway platform posed a few problems of its own. This had to be thinly constructed, yet stiff enough to carry the corrugated covering and also be capable of having the trusses that show prominently at its ends fixed to it. In addition, it needed to be located at the correct loading gauge clearance to enable rolling stock to pass beneath it. Having dismissed the use of plastic card for being too flexible and then thin plywood on the grounds of being more difficult to attach various other materials to, I eventually decided to make the bulk of its structure from brass.

I started by cutting the main slope from a sheet of 10thou thick brass sheet from the Metal Centre range, with a cut out in front of the upper doors to accommodate the hoist position. To this I soldered four strips of scrap rail to provide both rigidity and a means of fixing the canopy to the main building once it was complete. Next, a strip of brass was soldered to the front edge to represent the fascia and to this was added a length of fine channel for the box gutter. Before I made the trusses up from fine section brass strip, I covered the whole of the upper surface with individual sheets of Ambis Engineering corrugated iron, in much the same way as I did earlier on the main roof areas

Unlike some of my other models, the creamery was pretty straightforward to paint. With a slightly weathered matt white base for the render and matt brick red walls elsewhere, the only other areas of colour were the green doors and fascias and the streaked grey corrugated sheets and dark grey flat roofs. The only real problem I had while painting was to try and hold such a massive model while trying to apply paint into some of the finer areas.

## Conclusion

Ok, so this building became in its latter stages a bit too large to handle for my liking (I still prefer to make much smaller stone-built cottages with fluffy roofs). That's a personal thing I suppose, in any case the problem was not insurmountable and with a bit of care and patience, it all came together in the end. I found that the planning and information-gathering stages in making this model were half the battle and if I am honest, my favourite bit of the job, (is that the quantity surveyor in me coming out I wonder?). Perhaps the project does, however, prove to the reader that almost any building is 'makeable' if you really want it. All I have really done in making the creamery is to break down a somewhat large and complicated structure into a number of reasonably straightforward elements that, let's face it, almost any reader with a bit of skill could do. The moral I suppose is not to be put off by something that is outwardly awkward, take your time and most of all enjoy what you are doing – well this is a hobby after all!

Moreton-in-Marsh creamery as it is today.

# THATCHED ROOFS

Bluebell Row on the author's Paston Ridings layout is based on prototypes from Dogsthorpe in Peterborough.

Thatching, up to the seventeenth century was, in fact, the most common type of roof covering found in most towns and villages across the country. Since then, this cheap, light and readily available material has been largely displaced by more durable, maintenance-free and less combustible alternatives. Thankfully, albeit in mostly rural areas, thatched buildings still survive in large numbers and can often be seen from the train window as you pass by.

Now I know many railway modellers would love to have a go at thatching but imagine, for some reason or another, they consider that the process is far to difficult or time consuming for the ordinary man in the street to attempt. Believe me it isn't! I only had a go because I was in plaster for ten months in the early 1980s

with a broken leg and read an article in a magazine that had been lent to me by Dave Smith, which featured his article on scratch-building Gresley coaches. As with any other project, I took the 'if they can do it so can I' approach and was soon making a mess, as I experimented with scraps of old material and tried to learn the ropes by making a fluffy roof. The 'Green Man' was, I will readily admit, a bit too complicated and was probably not the best choice for a first attempt, but it still takes pride of place on the layout and, as you will have already seen, in the pages of this book too.

If you look around, you will find that there are actually three main types of thatching in use today; namely long straw, Norfolk reed and combed wheat reed. From the model-makers point of

view, both the Norfolk and combed wheat reed types are aligned with just the tips of the reed bundles showing on the face of the roof, whereas long straw thatch is aligned such that the bundles follow the roof slope down to the eaves. Another way to spot the difference is that dormers and features in a long straw thatch have a much softer appearance. Roofs of this type also have to be bound along the bottom edge, and often on the sides as well, by bindings usually made from hazel, known as liggers. Being denser in composition, the two reed types do not need any additional binding and the dormers and detailing are much crisper in appearance. In the past the type of thatch used was, to a great extent, governed by locality to the

**1.** Alwalton post office captured whilst still thatched in long straw.

**2.** This butcher's shop illustrates a modern decorative style of thatching.

**3.** A plain thatch at Oakhan in Rutland.

**4** A typical Devon thatch is captured at picturesque Cockington near Torquay.

**5.** This thatched pub can be found right in Spalding's town centre.

**6.** This small thatched church would make an ideal model.

source of its materials. Today limitations on availability, planning regulations and financial considerations also apply, particularly as a reed thatch will last about twice as long as a straw one. As a basic rule all three types work around a minimum roof pitch of around 50°.

To make a thatched building in 4mm scale, the main thing you need to source is a hank of plumber's hemp. Don't be put off by those who say you just can't get it any more. I haven't had a problem buying it from a plumber's merchant over the years and, in the last few weeks, even noticed some on sale in my local B&Q! The only other piece of specialist equipment, if you can call them that, is a pair of curved scissors – mine are 'Fiskars' bought from the haberdashery department of John Lewis.

Plumber's hemp is the raw material used to model thatch.

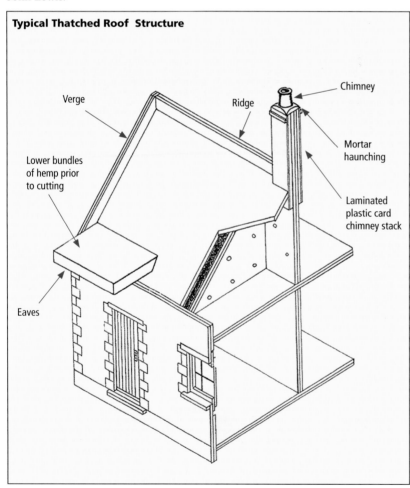

**Typical Thatched Roof Structure**

Verge

Ridge

Chimney

Lower bundles of hemp prior to cutting

Mortar haunching

Laminated plastic card chimney stack

Eaves

## A Simple Thatched Roof

Having made the basic shell of your building and prepared a plastic sub-roof, the first job when it comes to thatching a model is to glue what I call a base layer in place along the eaves of the roof. This comprises bundles of hemp approximately 5mm in diameter and about 15mm long which are, in turn, dipped into a tin lid containing 'Evo-Stick' contact adhesive, so that a liberal amount coats just the tips of the bundles, making sure that all the ends of the hemp fibres are covered. (I dab the bundles into a thin layer of glue spread onto the tin lid, to ensure I get just the right amount of glue on the hemp.) Starting at one corner, these bundles are fixed, one at a time, on the bottom edge of the roof as depicted by the accompanying photographs.

While the glue is still wet, the hemp bundles at the ends of the row need to be fanned out in such a way as to ensure that the tips of the fibres will show along the verge once the hemp is cut to shape. Now repeat the process until the hemp bundles have been positioned all of the way along the eaves of both roof slopes.

Don't forget to check that they are fully bonded to the roof structure and roughly in alignment as you do so. Despite your eagerness and enthusiasm to carry on thatching, set the model aside to allow the adhesive to dry out fully. I have found, from bitter experience, that a roof can be covered in hemp, layer after layer, from the bottom right to the top but, horror of horrors, when you press some of the upper layers of hemp in place, the wet glue holding the lower rows can give way, causing the whole roof to slump. Although on that occasion I just managed to rectify matters in time, I resolved not to repeat the mistake on subsequent models by employing a small dollop of patience. I now let the bottom layer dry thoroughly, so it acts as a firm foundation for the rest.

As the glue hardens, so to speak, it is well worth mentioning a little more about my choice of adhesive for sticking the hemp to the roof base. When I first started thatching I always used good old-fashioned 'Evo-Stick'. Being a quick drying contact adhesive, I found it ideal for sticking hemp to both plastic and plywood roof bases. Its pretty pungent odour however, makes it fairly unpleasant to work with for prolonged periods of time and is definitely a health-hazard if you don't use it in a well-ventilated environment. Largely due to the strong smell and obvious health risks of this adhesive I eventually started to look around for suitable alternatives.

The first I tried for a while was the modeller's favourite, white PVA previously known as 'Resin W' wood glue. Although I had to stick a thin sheet of plywood over my plastic roof slopes before I could use it, I found the results pretty good and used it for a number of my models. At that time, the only problems I encountered with the pva is that it readily penetrates the hemp fibres causing them to stick together (usually just where you don't want them to). If, for one reason or another, you get too much glue on a bundle, you can end up with patches of roof where stuck together hemp is

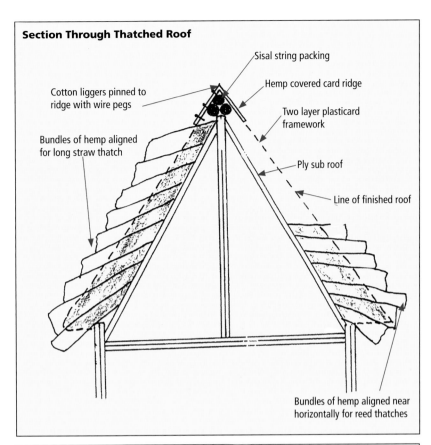

**Section Through Thatched Roof**

Sisal string packing

Hemp covered card ridge

Cotton liggers pinned to ridge with wire pegs

Two layer plasticard framework

Bundles of hemp aligned for long straw thatch

Ply sub roof

Line of finished roof

Bundles of hemp aligned near horizontally for reed thatches

**1.** The first row of hemp is stuck along the eaves.

**2.** This is then repeated on the other side of the model.

**3.** A few more rows of hemp are added.

**4.** The process continues steadily up the roof.

Paston Ridings thatched Post Office is based on a prototype from Alwalton near Peterborough.

exposed once the cutting process has taken place. With sparing use of the glue however, this problem was easily eliminated. The only other slight drawback of PVA is that the drying time is considerably longer than for the 'Impact' adhesive I had previously used.

My favoured product these days is the solvent-free 'Evo-Stick', a non-volatile, water based contact adhesive that is now on the market as an alternative to its smellier predecessor. I find this is an excellent glue, as it does not penetrate the hemp as easily as PVA, has no foul smell whilst in use and can be easily cleaned up when spilled. When compared with the solvent based 'Impact' adhesive the drying time is definitely longer, but is nowhere near as long as the PVA glue.

Right, back to the roof! Now that the bottom layer has had a chance to harden, the rest of the thatched roof can be covered. The method is, yes you've guessed it, exactly the same as for the base layer – cut a bundle, dip the end in adhesive and stick it in place – repeated lots and lots of times. The

only thing you have to remember is that fanning out the bundles forms the sides of the thatching at both the verges and dormer windows, pretty much as mentioned earlier. I know this process does sound a bit tedious, but it really is very simple to do and, once you've had a bit of practice, doesn't take that long. To make the task in hand less of a chore, I usually cut a quantity of the hemp bundles before I begin and space them out on an old tea tray. As I use each one in turn, I simply trim off any odd bits and glue them to the roof of my model. When the whole roof is covered, you end up with a shaggy cottage that closely resembles 'Dougal' from *The Magic Roundabout* rather than a scale model of a thatched building. Put this aside to dry out thoroughly, 24 hours or more is advisable.

Cutting and trimming the roof is the make or break element of thatching a model. Get it right and you will have a decent model, get it wrong and you will probably have to strip it all off and start again.

Many people often have the misconception that model thatches can be shaved or trimmed to length with electric hair clippers in a couple of minutes. In reality, the only effective way is to hand-cut the hemp using a couple of pairs of good quality sharp scissors and the experience gained from a few hours of practice. To this end, I would recommend any newcomer to thatching to make up a simple roof structure from plastic card and try out all of the stages described in these pages as a learning exercise. If need be, have two or three trial runs before starting thatching a model for real - I seem to remember messing around with an old Airfix kit when I first decided to have a go.

Essentially, the cutting process starts in the bottom right-hand corner of each roof slope and works upwards to the ridge bit-by-bit, gradually moving towards the left in so doing. I suppose the opposite cutting strategy might be better if you are left-handed, assuming of course that you can get the scissors to cut this way round. Before you begin, take the curved scissors and, if necessary, sharpen them on a fine grade stone. As you can see from the photos, the first few cuts set out the slope that will be followed across the whole of the roof. Cutting upwards, trim away a small amount of the oversized hemp roof, all the time checking for alignment of the roof slope, until you have a neat straight edge. Don't bother too much about the long hemp strands around the verge at this time; these will be tidied up later.

Now that you have started, you will have soon learnt the benefits of the curved scissors. The main advantage is that they can easily keep the line of cut parallel to the roof slope without cutting or digging in. If you tried to do the same with straight scissors you would almost certainly have trouble keeping the slope accurate, would find that they dig and take out chunks of hemp from areas of roof where you don't want them to.

Once the outer edge is to your liking, keep on trimming from bottom to top of the roof a millimetre or so into the 'haystack' at a time. Whatever you do don't be tempted to cut away too much in one go and always use the cut edge as a datum or template for the rest of the roof.

When trimming, the only area that needs special mention is the area of thatch above the dormer windows. Usually these tend to bulge out and sit slightly proud of the surrounding area. This, of course, depends on the prototype cottage and the area of country that it originates from, check your photos if you are uncertain. Once again, experience of a mock-up cottage roof is useful but not essential. Simply mark the rough position of the dormer area on the uncut roof with a marker pen and cut the fibres over this area so that they are slightly longer than their final length. This will then enable you to make a second cut over the dormer to shape and fine-tune the area.

Now that the roof slope has been trimmed, and the whole process has been repeated on the other side, you can take a bit of time tidying up any rough or long

**5.** One roof slope has been covered in hemp.

**6.** The process starts on the other slope but between the dormer windows.

**7.** Eventually the whole roof is covered.

**8.** The cutting process begins.

**9.** A rough profile for the completed roof is cut into the thatch.

**10** Cutting then continues across the roof.

**11.** Special care has to be taken around the dormers.

**12.** The thatch has been cut and awaits final trimming and tidying up.

areas of the thatch. To do this, I find a quick way of revealing any longer areas of hemp is to simply rub a finger in an upwards direction over the roof. In so doing, the longer strands will be seen to lie slightly proud of the rest, this will allow them to be carefully trimmed away before the fibres are brushed back downwards into their normal resting position.

To finish off the main roof covering, take some small straight scissors and start to cut away the excess hemp around the dormer windows, eaves and verges. As elsewhere, keep referring to your trusty set of photographs and remember not to trim too much away at a time. Keep on snipping away bit-by-bit, until all of the borders look neat and tidy. Unlike elsewhere on the roof, I usually use the straight scissors for most of the edge trimming, but I do find that there are some more awkward places that are best attacked with the curved ones.

Although I certainly wouldn't recommend a particularly complicated shaped roof to an inexperienced model-maker, the basic principles of these models are just the same whatever you

A completed thatched cottage.

do. Where you have two roof slopes meeting, such as at a valley, it is essential that one of the slopes is covered, trimmed and finished off before the adjoining one is started. The accompanying sketch gives an indication of how to plan such a roof and depicts the order in which the thatch should be completed. If you spend a few moments planning your roof before you begin, all hopefully will become clear and any potential problems will be raised.

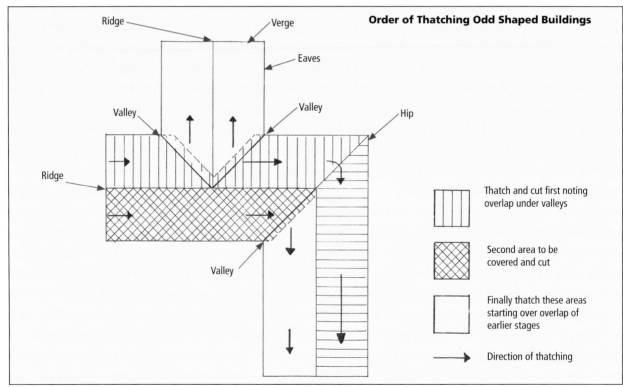

This 'aerial' view of Royal Oak cottage clearly shows its unusual shape.

## Finishing Touches

Although I have tried several different ways of making ridges, the method I prefer nowadays is to form a semi-solid ridge base using a few rows of sisal string that is glued to the top of the roof slopes. Next I make the ridge proper by marking it out on a piece of thin card that has been folded double along its apex. Having cut this out with a sharp knife, I then take some thin bundles of hemp and carefully glue them over the card ridge, taking care not to end up with a soaked mat of fibres that will look odd on the completed model. Once this has been allowed to dry any waste hemp can soon be trimmed away and the completed ridge can be fixed to the model using PVA glue making sure that it is both square and level in so doing. Don't worry about any loose strands of

Well Cottage  has a modern decorative ridge featuring scallops and points.

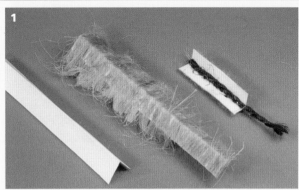

**1.** Various stages of ridge construction.

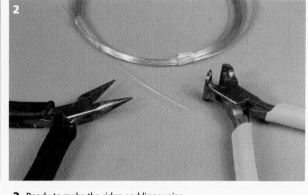

**2.** Ready to make the ridge and ligger pins.

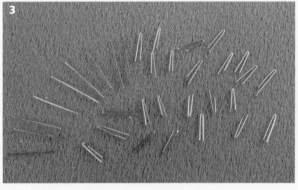

**3.** The tiny pins are ready to model the liggers or runners.

**4.** A completed section of ridge.

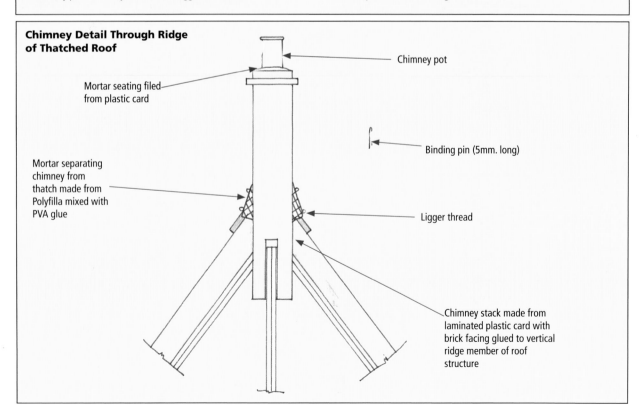

**Chimney Detail Through Ridge of Thatched Roof**

Chimney pot

Mortar seating filed from plastic card

Binding pin (5mm. long)

Mortar separating chimney from thatch made from Polyfilla mixed with PVA glue

Ligger thread

Chimney stack made from laminated plastic card with brick facing glued to vertical ridge member of roof structure hemp that you might have, these will shortly be held in place by the liggers and you can trim any odd bits up later.

To make liggers, which are found on both the ridges of all and perimeters of many thatches, you first need to bend up small pegs, very similar to miniature hairgrips, from fine wire. These can easily be driven into the thatch around lengths of thread that represent the liggers itself. Once you are happy that the liggers are accurately positioned, a tiny spot of PVA glue will soon secure each peg in place.

It is worth noting that the layout and pattern of the liggers, or runners, as they are sometimes known, varies tremendously from cottage to cottage. Some just have simple parallel rows across the ridge and others involve ornate decorative patterns commonly featuring scallops and points. Having studied many photos, it would appear that plain designs were more common in the past when the humble thatched cottage was lived in by the less affluent and the modern trend for intricate decoration had not so widely evolved. If, like me, you fancy a decorative style, all you have to do is use several strands of thread and weave them in and out of the pegs until the prototypical pattern has been replicated.

The only thing left to complete the roof, with of course the exception of painting, is to make a mortar surround to any chimney stacks. To do this just take a small amount of Polyfilla, add a spot of pva glue and mix it to a fairly stiff paste before carefully filling in the gap around the chimney using a cocktail stick or the end of an old needle file as an applicator.

LEFT: This detail shows a decorative ridge under construction.

RIGHT: A completed decorative ridge showing the mortar around a chimney stack.

St Paul's Row was built using information gleaned from old photographs and postcards.

The completed model.

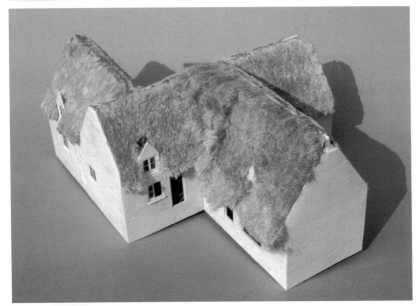

The Royal Oak under construction.

Royal Oak cottage is actually based on the pub of the same name, just a few miles along the old route of the A47 from Wansford Road station, in the Cambridgeshire village of Castor.

Although when I modelled this prototype I didn't stick rigidly to the 1930s period (as can be seen by the highly decorative ridge), the building does feature an odd shaped roof, attractive dormer windows and has a bay window with a Collyweston slate roof.

Regular readers of *British Railway Modelling* may remember this model featuring on the front cover of the very first issue back in April 1993.

The prototype in the village of Castor.

This terraced row is pictured during the painting process.

As most scratch-built models consist of white plastic card, it is pretty easy to paint straight onto the surface as it comes, with no priming or surface treatment being necessary. If you have any doubts, or simply just want to remove any greasy traces left by handling, you can, if you wish, lightly wash and rub the outer surface of the walls using a little old fashioned scouring powder dampened on a toothbrush. Always be very careful to avoid the whole model becoming wet as you rinse away the residue and especially avoid water getting in contact with any hemp or paper surfaces. If you have used grey or red embossed plastic card to make brick walls and you need to paint the surface a much lighter colour, mask off the area taking care to cover and seal any windows so that you can

apply a thin coat of acrylic white spray car primer to act as a base. Where you have large expanses of light cream or yellow brickwork, why not spray a whole embossed sheet before you use it? This will certainly save a fair bit of time later.

With the surface prepared, there are two main types of paint that are best suited to colouring plastic sheets. These are enamels and acrylics. I find that the type of paint you use is largely based upon experience. My preference has always been for enamels, as I have always used them since I was young. Other modellers will say the same about their acrylic counterparts. Whichever you use, get yourself a good selection of matt colours to suit more or less any building that you might wish to make. Despite painted wood being predominantly finished in gloss, a glossy

finish on a model looks horrible and out of place, so try satin paints instead for a more subtle finish on these surfaces.

When it comes to mixing paint, I use an old scrap plastic food tray as a palette and always have a supply of clean white spirit handy for thinning enamels (and some dirty white spirit for cleaning brushes as well). It is probably worth getting a selection of reasonable quality brushes and a couple of thicker flat ones for dry brushing and weathering. Pinch a kitchen roll from the domestic authority for cleaning and wiping and you are ready to get started.

As nearly all buildings have an uneven, weathered appearance, I find it best to place well-stirred splodges of various colours on the palette and mix away until I get something that approximates the desired hue. If you don't fully mix the colours together you can, with a bit of practice, get some pretty convincing effects on brick and stone surfaces. As with other aspects of model-making, always try out the paint finish on a mock-up or some plastic card offcuts, after all these can be thrown away if they are not right and will not ruin hours of time and effort spent creating a one off scratch-built structure.

Having treated the walls and let them dry thoroughly you can, if the prototype dictates, apply touches of colour to represent any special details that may exist and also pick out the mortar between the brick courses. To do this, brush the surface of the painted walls with a generous coat of water making sure that it goes into all of the joints. Then, before the water dries out, take a very weak mix of grey paint (thinned white emulsion with a few spots of black and a spot or two of washing up liquid to reduce the surface tension), load your brush and simply touch the wall where a number of bricks meet. Capillary action instantaneously draws the grey paint quite a way into the dampened joints. To cover a whole building, you have to repeat the process several times, wiping away any excess paint as you go along. Now although I have described how to do this you may have already spotted that I find this effect a little too overstated and very rarely use this technique on my own models. Take a good look around and, more often as not, you will find that walls have been built with a mortar that is sympathetically coloured to match the facing bricks, or that the contrasting mortar has become much weathered and toned down over time.

Unlike the painting of locos and rolling stock, my airbrush sees very little action when it comes to model buildings. The only places where it does see use are for large expanses of corrugated roofing (that have already been primed with car primer) and to apply the basic colour, and indeed some subtle tones, to my thatched roofs. In both instances the models are thoroughly masked with

Thatched roofs can be masked with newspaper and finished using an airbrush.

both newspaper and tape first.

Once all of the solid colours have been added, try a little dry brushing to represent the weathering of the walls, taking care to consult prototype photos wherever possible as you do so. I often take a look at Martyn Welch's informative book on the subject to refresh my memory and pick up a few new tips and ideas.

## Finishing Touches

Now that your building is nearing completion, it is time to think about adding any special adornments or features that the prototype might have. If you look very carefully, you will often find that there are a whole host of interesting

little details that will add character and that all important finishing touch to your scratch-built structure.

Embellishments such as built-in letter boxes, air bricks or grilles and cast iron boot scrapers are commonly found on period properties, whereas practical additions such as lamps, signs and fire buckets frequently add interest to buildings of a more railway nature.

Having just mentioned lamps, it is well worth adding that many modellers like to light up their buildings with miniature LEDs, grain-of-wheat bulbs or even fibre optics. If you are one such modeller, it is a good idea, I reckon, to line the inside of the walls so that light doesn't stray

The interior of the Gents' toilet on Wansford Road station building.

**1.** Post boxes can often be seen recessed into station walls.

**2.** Steps and handrails add interest to an entrance.

**3.** Behind the Bluebell Inn are a collection of outbuilding that were made by reference to old photos.

**4.** A typical boot scraper.

**5.** This boot scraper is fitted into a recess in the wall.

**6.** A round tie rod and spreader plate.

**7.** An ornate cast iron ventilation grille.

**8.** Mosaic tiles were a common feature at shop entrances.

**9.** A period doorbell push.

**10.** A typical pavement ventilation grille.

**11.** Fire buckets are commonly found on station walls.

through the translucent plastic card and spoil the whole effect. Although you can simply paint the inside of the model black as it is assembled, I have seen that some model makers prefer to line the walls with coloured card or even silver foil to enhance reflectance. If you do want to light up a building, try not to illuminate the whole structure, why not make things more realistic by only lighting up selective rooms, to give a prototypical hit-and-miss effect.

As a rule, I usually only elect to make room interiors where you can see in through a very large window or an open door. If you light up your buildings this extra detailing process may well be worth considering. The level of interior detailing you chose to add really depends upon the scale. In 7mm scale you can often see a lot of detail through an average window, whereas it is much more difficult to pick out too much of an interior from a similar sized window in 4mm scale. In the interior pictured, I have made a quick mock-up of a front room with an internal door and frame, skirtings, wainscot panelling, dado rail and a carpeted floor. To complete the scene, a painted white metal figure was strategically placed so that it would be seen through the cottage's open door. The whole thing is made to be a push fit inside the building and is easily removed if required.

Being open to view, the interior of the Gents toilet on my Wansford Road

**1.** Plastic strip soon makes tie rod spreader plates.

**2.** This canopy was made using an old pill container.

**3.** A boot scraper is an effective feature on an old building.

**4.** This chicken coop can be quickly scratch-built to enhance the rural scene.

station building was more of a necessity. Once again a simple plastic card interior was made to accommodate the obligatory chap having a pee. Similarly, shop window displays can be made from odd scraps of plastic card and section.

Moving outside the building itself, we inevitably find that the site is often populated by a whole host of sundry structures ranging from sheds and

stores to lean-to extensions, chicken coops and privvies. Quite often these are much less substantially built and can be usually modelled quite quickly using pretty much the same methods as we have already seen.

I know it might seem pretty obvious, but have a good look around you, model exactly what you see and your layout will soon mirror reality and hopefully come to life.

**5.** The Post Office's window display.

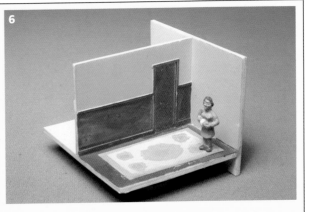

**6.** A simple cottage interior.

This scene depicts an M&GNR Class A 4-4-2T passing through Paston Ridings village.

Hopefully, as this insight into the basics of scratch-building model buildings comes to an end, the reader, whether just starting to scratch-build structures for the first time or not, will have gleaned a few useful tips from my scribblings. Indeed, I hope that they will have seen that this type of model making is really a lot simpler than he or she may at first imagine, and be inspired to have a go. I know I say it time and time again, but almost any technique is one of firstly finding out what to do and secondly having the confidence to get started. If you don't feel happy that you can get something right, don't be afraid to try it out on a mock-up before

you attempt it on your chosen prototype. I very often try out new ideas and methods and, if I hadn't spilled the beans here, nobody would ever know. If need be, why not use old scraps of materials and experiment away? You too will, I hope, have that same rewarding sense of achievement when something outwardly tricky goes right.

If you have never scratch-built a building before why not start with something simple? There are plenty of sheds and outbuildings out there along our railways that are ideal topics for you to cut your scratch-building teeth on. Ok, so I know I picked a couple of quite complicated prototypes to start

with, but that's me all over – call it youthful exuberance or something – well it was almost thirty years ago! Why not pick out something to model, buy some materials and a few tools if you need them, and set to? I started, as I have already mentioned, purely out of necessity, but soon became hooked on model buildings. Indeed I had made a whole load of models before I put them all together in the form of the layout. Even the station was a later addition to the scope of things and is one of my more recent models. Although it is a while since I started my EM gauge layout 'Paston Ridings', I still have fresh ideas for new buildings

# The definitive collection with over 500 scale drawings of
# LNER locomotives, vans and coaches.

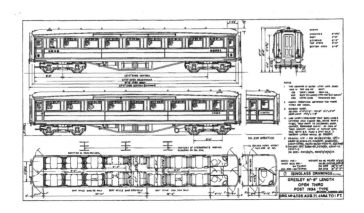

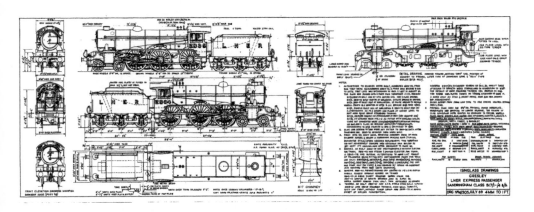

For prices and catalogue, please visit
www.Isinglass-Models.co.uk
Email Isinglass@Edgson.net
or write to:
Mrs. M. Edgson, 20 Gallants Farm Road,
East Barnet, Herts. EN4 8ET

# If the question is L.N.E.R.

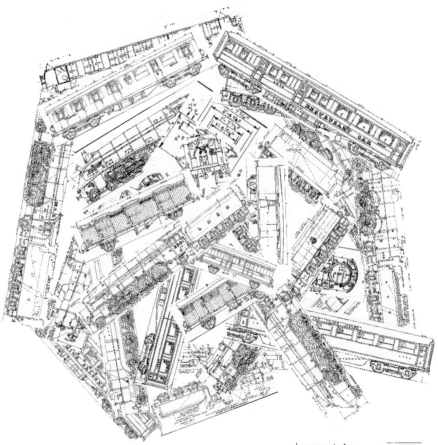

# Then the Answer is

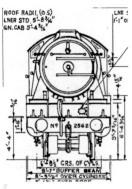

Eastwell Cottage.

and gaps left often become populated with new cottages.

If you need further inspiration, why not visit some of the larger shows? Or better still, look out for some of the fantastic layouts featured monthly in *British Railway Modelling*. Always look around you, take photos if you can, and you will soon discover that there is much more to model railways than just track laying and running trains.

Well, hopefully this book will have inspired a few readers to take the plunge and make their first steps in scratch-building. It may have given others, who haven't built anything for a while, the impetus to start something, or it may just shed a bit of light on a topic that has previously been a mystery. Whatever your interest, I hope you go on to enjoy this fascinating stream of the hobby as much as I have; always remember one very important thing, whatever you do – have fun!

A row of scratch-built thatched cottages.

# SCRATCH-BUILT BUILDINGS

| | Page No |
|---|---|
| Introduction | 2 |
| Why Scratch-Build? | 4 |
| Tools, Paints and Adhesives | 8 |
| Research, Surveying and Planning | 10 |
| Brickwork | 16 |
| Stonework | 30 |
| Rendered Walls | 42 |
| Timber Buildings | 46 |
| Windows and Doors | 56 |
| Assembling Your Building | 64 |
| Chimney Stacks | 70 |
| Slate and Tile Roofing | 76 |
| Corrugated and Flat Roofs | 84 |

This small thatched cottage was made in an attempt to learn the process of thatching in miniature.

| | |
|---|---|
| External Pipework and Guttering | 92 |
| Thatched Roofs | 100 |
| Painting and Finishing Touches | 112 |
| Moving Forward | 116 |

These buildings based on prototypes from Dogsthorpe in Peterborough are seen forming part of the village on the author's Paston Ridings layout.

# PROTOTYPE PROJECTS

|  | Page No |  |  |
| --- | --- | --- | --- |
| Shipston-on-Stour Engine Shed | 26 | Wansford Road Station | 74 |
| The Bluebell Inn | 40 | Shipston-on-Stour Goods Shed | 88 |
| Shipston-on-Stour Station | 52 | Moreton-in-Marsh Creamery | 96 |
|  |  | Royal Oak Cottage | 110 |

## The Thank You Bit

As is customary, there are a few people who I would like to thank for their help in the making of this book. Firstly I must mention the Head of Production and Design, Jayne Thorpe for her help and assistance; Designer Andrianna Curtis for setting out of the book and putting my pictures and words in exactly the right places; *BRM's* Managing Editor David Brown for buying me a pint; *BRM's* John Emerson and Richard Wilson for reading over; Publisher John Greenwood and his boss Stephen Warner for allowing me to write a second book in the series (it is a pity that Stephen's dad, Michael, isn't still around to see his buildings in print again) and once again 'the boss' for her tolerance whilst I am making my usual mess modelling.

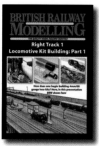

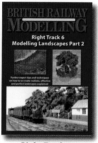

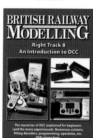

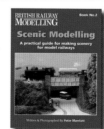